THE RISES AND FALLS OF MAN – DESTINY – 3000 AD
NEW SUPPORT FOR A SUPERORGANISM MACRO-THEORY OF CIVILIZATIONS FROM CURRENT WORLD TRENDS AND NEW PERUVIAN, PRE-MAYAN, MAYAN, ANATOLIAN, AND EARLY EGYPTIAN DATA, WITH A PROJECTION TO 3000 AD

STEPHEN BLAHA

The Rises and Falls of Man – Destiny – 3000 AD
New Support for a Superorganism Macro-Theory of Civilizations From Current World Trends and New Peruvian, Pre-Mayan, Mayan, Anatolian, and Early Egyptian Data, with a Projection to 3000 AD

Stephen Blaha

Blaha Research

Copyright © 2014 by Stephen Blaha. All Rights Reserved.

This document is protected under copyright laws and international copyright conventions. No part of this book may be reproduced, stored in a retrieval system, or transmitted by any means in any form, electronic, mechanical, photocopying, recording, or as a rewritten passage(s), or otherwise, without the express prior written permission of Blaha Research. For additional information write to

Blaha Research, P. O. Box 368, Auburn, NH 03032 USA

ISBN: 978-0-9893826-1-8

This document is provided "as is" without a warranty of any kind, either implied or expressed, including, but not limited to, implied warranties of fitness for a particular purpose, merchantability, or non-infringement. This document may contain typographic errors, technical inaccuracies, and may not describe recent developments. This book is printed on acid free paper.

Cover Credit

A symbolic representation of the transition of American pyramids from early days (bottom pyramid) to Classical Mayan (top pyramid) with the flags of some current major powers whose actions remind the author of the recurrent warfare between Classical Mayan city-states.

© Copyright 2014 by Stephen Blaha. All Rights Reserved.

Rev. 00/00/01   August 25, 2014

To My Wife Margaret

Some Other Books by Stephen Blaha

The Rhythms of History: A Universal Theory of Civilizations (Pingree-Hill Publishing. Auburn, NH, 2002).

The Life Cycle of Civilizations (Pingree-Hill Publishing. Auburn, NH, 2002).

A Unified Quantitative Theory Of Civilizations and Societies: 9600 BC - 2100 AD (Pingree-Hill Publishing. Auburn, NH, 2004).

SuperCivilizations: Civilizations as Superorganisms (McMann-Fisher Publishing, Auburn, NH, 2010).

All the Universe! Faster Than Light Tachyon Quark Starships & Particle Accelerators with the LHC as a Prototype Starship Drive Scientific Edition (Pingree-Hill Publishing, Auburn, NH, 2011).

Multi-Stage Space Guns, Micro-Pulse Nuclear Rockets, and Faster-Than-Light Quark-Gluon Ion Drive Starships (Blaha Research, Auburn, NH, 2013).

All the Multiverse! Starships Exploring the Endless Universes of the Cosmos using the Baryonic Force (Blaha Research, Auburn, NH, 2014)

Universes and Multiverses: From a New Standard Model to a Physical Multiverse; The Big Bang; Our Sister Universe's Wormhole; Origin of the Cosmological Constant, Spatial Asymmetry of the Universe, and its Web of Galaxies; A Baryonic Field between Universes and Particles; Flatverse Extended Wheeler-DeWitt Equation (Blaha Research, Auburn, NH, 2014)

Available on bn.com, Amazon.com, Amazon.co.uk and other international web sites as well as at better bookstores (through Ingram Distributors).

Preface

Recent events have created a changed international scene that reflects the projections of our macro-theory of civilizations in our books of 2001 - 2010. This book presents data that shows the current state of the world is consistent with our theory. It further shows that recently discovered archaeological data for many regions of the world also agree with our theory.

We begin with a study of major changes in the world situation since our first theoretical results were published in 2002. The changes clearly agree with our theory's predictions – although only a brief period has elapsed since we made them. We predicted that Russia, China, Islam, and India would be in a rapid growth phase until later in the 21st century while Japan and Western civilization (particularly the United States – the leading Western nation) were in a declining phase. The United States and Western civilization are expected to begin growth again around 2050 in our theory.

These cycles of change will continue into the future and create a very different world situation within the next hundred years irrespective of the changes due to global warming that have been featured in the press for many years. The changes have extremely important consequences for the future. This book analyzes the current and projected situation of the four current major players: the United States, Russia, China and India as well as Japan and Islam. We find that they all conform to the predictions of our theory.

We also make a long term prediction of the world situation in the year 3000 AD together with an analysis of potential major events that could influence the evolution of civilizations over the next thousand years.

The picture that emerges is not a pretty one for the West, or for the world in general, if the world population remains large. It is clear that universal prosperity with a standard of living comparable to that of the present United States is unattainable without a sharp reduction in the world's population. The political ramifications and the effects of such a reduction would be enormous.

After studying the current and future of world civilizations we turn to past civilizations for which new data has recently appeared. This new data for Peruvian, Pre-Mayan, Mayan, Anatolian, and Early pre-pyramids Egyptian civilization is in clear agreement with our theory.

In the past two years important field work studies of Mayan civilizations have appeared on the origins of Pre-Classical Mayan civilization, and the rises and falls of Classical Mayan civilization.

In 2012, Kennett et al studied climate change from 300 AD to 1000 AD and obtained an understanding of the climate of Classical Mayan times including the period in which it ended. Their climate data is in good agreement with our theory's Mayan civilization growth curve as it should be since our theory is based on the energetics of growth due to resource acquisition and utilization. Our theory describes the cyclic rises and falls of Classical Mayan civilization. Remarkably there is a strong correlation between the climate data of Kennett et al and our cyclic pattern of Classical Mayan civilization.

In 2002 we proposed a civilization theory that, when applied to the Maya, implied that the Mayans had a sequence of two successive civilizations: Pre-Classical Mayan civilization and Classical Mayan civilization. Pre-Classical Mayan civilization extended from approximately 1168 BC to approximately 250 BC; Classical Mayan civilization lasted from about 223 BC to 900 AD.

In 2013, Inomata et al investigated the origins of lowland Mayan civilization in the period from 1000 BC to 700 BC. They found that the origins of the Mayan civilizations (Pre-Classical Mayan and Classical Mayan) were primarily from Chiapas, the Pacific coast, and the southern Gulf Coast.

We attributed the origin of Pre-Classical Mayan civilization in part to the significant influence of fishing fleets of Andean civilizations from Ecuador and Peru. Inomata et al have apparently confirmed the impact of Andean civilizations on Mayan origins. A major point in favor of this concept is the appearance of Andean artifacts at points along the coast up as far as Chiapas, Mexico. A more impressive point is the first appearance of a pyramidal structure in Central America at Ocós on the Guatemalan coast not far from Cival. This structure, seemingly suggested by fishermen/trader visitors from Ecuador and Peru, is very likely the prototype for the later pyramids of the Mayans. Thus our theory of Pre-Classical Mayan civilization has strong field support for its origins.

Thus in addition to the close match of our theory to 50 odd other civilizations in Africa, Asia and Europe described in earlier books, we find a detailed match between our theory and important new data on Mayan civilizations.

In this book we first examine the broad features of our theory and then the theory's implications for the present and 3000 AD.

Then we consider Peruvian (Andean) civilizations and show that they propagate in two paths from their origin at Caral due to the linear coastal geography of Peru and Ecuador. In particular we describe new data of Covey et al on the Wari civilization that supports our view of an Andean chain of civilizations.

After noting the propagation of civilizations in the Americas we discuss the more complex two-dimensional propagation of civilizations in Anatolia. We show the new data on Göbekli Tepe, the world's oldest monumental temple, and the center of a hunter-gatherer proto-civilization, suggests (Dr. Giulio Magli) that it was designed for the worship and tracking of the Dog Star, Sirius. Since large observatory construction and astronomical study are civilizational activities we find evidence for a hunter-gatherer proto-civilization as predicted in our earlier work.

We also predicted the existence of a predecessor civilization, Nile River civilization, to the known pyramid building Egyptian civilization. New work (Michael Dee et al) has established the lineage of the Nile River civilization rulers. It is the same (with one addition) as our theory with historical events that are consistent with our growth curve for Nile River civilization. Further, another study (Jana Jones et al) has shown that mummification methods were the same in both civilizations. Since Death was of great importance in Egyptian culture the continuity of the mummification process between the civilizations supports the status of Nile River civilization as the predecessor of the well-known Egyptian civilization.

Thus we have a civilization macro-theory that is in agreement with the present and the past, and confirmed by new data.

.

CONTENTS

1. A DETERMINISTIC THEORY OF CIVILIZATIONS 1

   1.1 Superorganism Theory of Civilizations, and of Social Insects and Other Species .. 2
      1.1.1 Superorganisms and Supercivilizations 3
      1.1.2 Examples of Superorganisms 4
      1.1.3 Perfect vs. Imperfect Superorganisms 5
         1.1.3.1 An Imperfect Superorganism Example 5
         1.1.3.2 Civilizations as Imperfect Superorganisms 6
   1.2 Energetic Principles For the Evolution of Superorganisms and Supercivilizations 7
   1.3 Evolution based on the Energetics/Thermodynamics of Civilizations 10
   1.4 A Deterministic Theory of Civilizations Exists 11
   1.5 Free Will and Our Rigorous Macro-Theory of Civilizations 12

NEW SUPPORT FOR A SUPERORGANISM
MACRO-THEORY OF CIVILIZATIONS
FROM CURRENT WORLD TRENDS

2. THE AGREEMENT BETWEEN OUR SUPERCIVILIZATION THEORY AND CURRENT TRENDS 14

   2.1 Our Theory's Predictions in Blaha (2002a) 14
   2.2 Overall Civilizational Trends and Events Consistent with Our Theory 21
      Technic (Western) 21
      Russian 22
      China 22
      India 22
      Japan 22
      Islamic 22
   2.3 Are there any Points of Disagreement? 23

3. MAJOR HAZARDS FACING THE WORLD TODAY 24

   3.1 Major World Epidemic Causing the Death of 25% -70% of Humanity 24
   3.2 A Major Nuclear War 25
   3.3 Civil Unrest, Corruption and Violence 27

3.4 Financial Collapse 29
3.5 Environmental Deterioration 29
3.6 Tectonic or Asteroid Disasters 30

4. 3000 AD BASED ON THE TREND OF WORLD CIVILIZATIONS 31

4.1 Social Nature of the Earth's Population in 3000 AD 31
4.2 Economic Conditions in 3000 AD 35
    4.2.1 Present World Economic Situation 35
    4.2.2 Environmental Conditions 36
    4.2.3 Zero Sum World Economy Today. The Future? 37
    4.2.4 The Effect of a Declining Population in the Next Thousand Years 38
    4.2.5 Waste Management in 3000 AD 39
    4.2.6 Increased Maintenance and Rebuilding Costs 39
4.3 Technology in 3000 AD 39
    4.3.1 New Advances Based on New More Powerful Computers 40
    4.3.2 Miniaturization of Devices and Artifacts 40
    4.3.3 Degradable Packaging 40
    4.3.4 Improved Cleanup Methods for Accumulated (Toxic) Waste 40
    4.3.5 A Possible Decline of Science and Technology 41
4.4 Civilizational/Political Conditions in 3000 AD 41
    4.4.1 A Continuation of Existing Civilizations? 42
    4.4.2 An End to Man's Expansion? 43
4.5 Exhaustion of Natural Resources? 43
4.6 The Increasing Probability of a Pandemic 44

**NEW SUPPORT FOR THE SUPERORGANISM
MACRO-THEORY OF CIVILIZATIONS
FROM NEW PERUVIAN, PRE-MAYAN, MAYAN, ANATOLIAN,
AND EARLY EGYPTIAN DATA**

5. NEW ARCHAEOLOGICAL DATA SUPPORTING OUR MACRO-THEORY 47

6. NEW DATA FOR PRE-CLASSICAL AND CLASSICAL MAYAN CIVILIZATIONS 48

6.1 Weather Data for Classical Mayan Civilization Supporting the Energetic Basis of the Theory and its Predictions for Classical Mayan Civilization 48

    Central America: Classical Mayan: 223 BC – 900 AD 48
  6.2 New Support for a Link between Peruvian Civilizations and Pre-Classical Mayan Civilization **53**
    Central America: Pre-Classical Mayan: 1168 BC – 250 BC 53

7. NEW DATA FOR PERUVIAN CIVILIZATIONS 60

  Moche (Mochica) Civilization, Northern Peru: 400 BC? – 750 AD 63
  Sequence II of Peruvian Civilizations: Caral, La Florida, Huari, Chincha, Inca 65
  Observations on Andean Geography 68
  7.1 New Data on the Huari (Wari) Civilization **68**

8. NEW DATA FOR ANATOLIAN CIVILIZATIONS 70

  8.1 Theory Applied to Early Anatolian Civilizations **70**
  8.2 New Data on Göbekli Tepe – One of the Earliest Known Civilized Sites **74**

9. NEW DATA FOR EARLY EGYPTIAN CIVILIZATION 75

  9.1 Early Egyptian Civilization **75**
    Nile River Civilization: 3691 BC – 2690 BC 75
  9.2 New Data on Early Egyptian (Nile River) Civilization - Rulers **80**
  9.3 New Data on Early Egyptian (Nile River) Civilization – Mummification **81**
  9.4 Support for Nile River Civilization **82**

REFERENCES 83
INDEX 87
ABOUT THE AUTHOR 91

FIGURES and TABLES

Table 1.1. Comparison of an organism with an insect superorganism. 3
Table 1.2. Comparison of a civilization with a superorganism. 6
Figure 1.1. The standard growth pattern of a 1,000 year lifetime civilization plotted against time. The zero point of time marks the beginning of the civilization. 8
Figure 1.2. The pattern of Hellenic Civilization with key events marked to show how they follow the trends of ups and downs of the civilization's growth curve which we call the Societal level S. The change in S (its derivative) is plotted as the curve C multiplied by 50. 9
Figure 31. A comparison of the phases of contemporary civilizations. The "earlier" phase is simply part of the period of a predecessor civilization before a startup begins. The predecessor may be similar to its successor. 15
Figure 6.6. Classical Mayan civilization growth/Societal Level compared to historical events. [The oscillating line is called the Societal level or Growth rate.] 49
Figure 6.1. A measure of rainfall patterns in Mayan times from Douglas J. Kennett et al, Science 338, 788 (2012). 51
Figure 6.2. A superposition of Figs. 6.1 and 6.6 above showing a correlation between rainfall and the growth rate of Classical Mayan civilization. 52
Figure 6.7. The growth/Societal Level of the Mayan sequence of civilizations with some Preclassic events shown. See Fig. 6.6 for the growth of Classical Mayan civilization and its events. 54
Figure 6.5. Trade route along the South and Central American coastline from Peru to Mexico with dates of Parita Bay (2130 BC) and Ocós (1500 BC) artifact finds indicated............................. 57
Figure 6.3. Major Pre-Classical Mayan sites. From Takeshi Inomata et al, Science 340, 467 (2013). 58
Figure 6.4. Map of Pre-Classical Mayan sites. From Takeshi Inomata et al, Science 340, 467 (2013). 59
Table 7.1. Caral Peruvian Civilization Growth Curve. 62
Figure 7.2. The Growth/Societal Level of Moche civilization compared to known events in Moche history... 64

v

Figure 7.3. Two sequences of civilizations: sequence I goes generally north from Caral; sequence II goes generally south from Caral. The Inca civilization grew from Cuzco to absorb all of the coast and highlands between northern Chile and Ecuador. 66

Figure 7.4. The growth/Societal Levels of the sequences: Caral, Casma, Moche and Chimú civilizations (black line labeled SI); and Caral, La Florida, Huari, Chincha, and Inca civilizations (white line labeled SII). 67

Figure 6.8. Early civilizations/societies in Neolithic, and Preneolithic, Anatolia. 71

Table 6.2. A table of some Neolithic and Chalcolithic civilizations. A number of others are not listed including Musular and Suberde. The dates for the Pre-Çatalhöyük layers are the "most likely" estimates from Hodder (2006) and are subject to change.. 72

Figure 9.1. Plot of growth/Societal Level S(t) (and the growth change function C(t) multiplied by fifty) for Egyptian civilization with historical events marked on the graph (from Blaha (2002).) The growth/Societal Level curve (eq. 8.9) is in good overall agreement with the trends of events.. 76

Figure 9.2. Growth/Societal Level curve of proposed Nile River civilization................................... 78

Figure 9.3. The Nile River and Egyptaic civilizations 3691 BC – 1000 BC growth/Societal Level curve S. 79

1. A Deterministic Theory of Civilizations

The historical evolution of civilizations has been a subject of speculation for at least 2500 years. Some ancient historians thought that civilizations followed a cyclic pattern. Modern historians have proposed a variety of patterns of civilizational evolution. Some have favored a cyclic pattern. Others have proposed other alternatives. In previous books we proposed a cyclic pattern with civilizations having a length of about 1,000 years if undisturbed by external events such as invasions. This pattern is subject to abrupt changes due to sudden major events in the history of a civilization. Major events could take the form of a sudden massive climatic or tectonic effect (e.g. volcanos), or an overwhelming conquest by another civilization (the most common occurrence). Our theory was documented, and verified in great detail, for over 50 civilizations, starting from the fourth millennium B.C., on all continents except Australia.

In developing a theory of civilizations it is important to distinguish between the major events in the history of each civilization and the (minor) transient events that do not significantly influence a civilization's overall evolution. The vagaries of human nature, natural events, and just plain chance events are not susceptible to a comprehensive theoretical analysis. Thus events may reflect the overall evolution of a civilization or they may not. The cumulative pattern of events in each stage of a civilization's evolution is capable of being interpreted in the context of a comprehensive theory of civilizations which we will call a macro-historical theory.

Civilizations seem to end in three ways: some civilizations simply expire dribbling down to a lower level of social organization; some civilizations end by being absorbed through conquest or by being overwhelmed culturally or technologically; some civilizations end through a major decline in their environment.[1]

---

[1] One of the best known examples of this type of decline appears to be the end of Classical Mayan civilization due to prolonged drought.

The well-documented pattern of rises and falls in civilizations, the often seen 1000 year lifetimes of isolated civilizations, and the mechanisms through which civilizations end, suggest that a macro-theory of civilizations is possible. Regularities in nature usually suggest an underlying mechanism is at play. In the next section we propose the mechanism for the evolution of civilizations is statistical in nature and based on the existence of resources to support a civilization and the ability of the people of a civilization to utilize them.

1.1 Superorganism Theory of Civilizations, and of Social Insects and Other Species

In Blaha (2002a) we presented a cyclic macro-theory of the history of civilizations and showed that it agreed with the history of many civilizations. The theory was phenomenological and it revealed a mathematical harmonic oscillator structure of ups and downs for civilizations. Many civilizations had abrupt changes due to conquests and environmental effects. But their successors resumed the cyclic behavior.

In Blaha (2010) we presented a theoretical foundation for our original cyclic theory of civilizations based on energetic principles.[2] *A fundamental physical basis for the evolution of civilizations gives us good reason to believe that we have a true theory – not just a set of theoretical or psychological conjectures as so many theories of history have tended to be.* We applied our theory to well over 50 civilizations in all parts of the world from approximately 3500 B. C. to the present. The agreement with macro-history was excellent. We also considered the impact of technology, environmental changes, and medical advances on civilizations.

Colonies of social insects such as bees and ants as well as bacterial colonies have been shown to conform to the energetic theory. Thus, following the terminology of superorganisms used for these species, we extended the term civilizations to the term supercivilizations to emphasize the unity of Nature in its dynamical processes of assemblages of plants and animals including Man.[3]

---

[2] The energetic principles are part of Thermodynamics – a general, fundamental theory of Physics. See section 1.2 for a description of these fundamental principles.
[3] The subsections below in small print were abstracted from Blaha (2010).

1.1.1 Superorganisms and Supercivilizations

The term superorganism,[4] defined as a social insect colony, was used by William M. Wheeler in Wheeler (1928). In 1911 he identified the features of an ant colony:[5]

1. It acts as a unit.
2. It has a unitary cycle of growth.
3. Its members show a variation in size and behavior that enables an identification of castes within the colony.
4. It has two major population groups: propagators (queens and mates), and workers.

The concept of insect superorganisms is well illustrated by Table 1.1, which displays the analogues of organisms and insect superorganisms.

Organism	Insect Superorganism
Cells	Individual insect members
Organs	Functional groups or castes
Sexual Organs	Reproduction group (queen(s) and mates)
Immune System	Danger communication & soldiers
Autoimmune and similar diseases	Conflicts between members for dominance
Somatic Organs	Worker groups
Circulatory System	Food and Information distribution system
Senses	External worker communications
Nervous System	Communications between members
Body (skin & skeleton)	The nest
Individual Growth & Development	Colony growth

Table 1.1. Comparison of an organism with an insect superorganism.

Some species of bees are also superorganisms. The reader is referred to Hölldobler (2009) for a detailed description, with excellent color pictures and illustrations, of insects and insect superorganisms.

---

[4] "The insect colony or society may be regarded as a super-organism and hence as a living whole …"
[5] With the statement, "The ant colony is an organism and not merely the analogue of the person."

1.1.2 Examples of Superorganisms

- **Insects**

Various ant and bee species are the best known types of superorganisms. The previous discussion gives only the barest details of the complexity of colonies of these species. The interested reader is directed to Hölldobler (2009) for a detailed exposition.

- **Microbes**

The list of superorganisms appears to be growing in dramatic ways. The New Scientist magazine (February 24, 2010) reports that Professor L. P. Nielsen of Aarhus University (Denmark) and colleagues have found evidence that sulfur-eating bacteria in muddy sediments on the ocean floor are connected by a network of microbial nanowires that enable communication via the exchange of electrons between the bacteria. This communication capability allows bacteria colonies to communicate over large distances and act as a superorganism. Professor Nielsen is quoted as saying, ""The discovery has been almost magic. It goes against everything we have learned so far. Micro-organisms can live in electric symbiosis across great distances. Our understanding of what their life is like, what they can and can't do - these are all things we have to think of in a different way now."

- **Other Types of Superorganisms**

It would be surprising if there were not many more types of superorganisms in nature. If species as diverse as insects and microbes can have superorganism behavior then it is likely other types of superorganisms are also very likely to exist. Some other possible superorganism candidates are:

- Buffalo Herds – Before the arrival of white men immense buffalo herds covering several Midwestern US states existed. The herds act in a synchronous fashion that suggests they may behave as superorganisms.
- Flocks of Birds
- Elephant Herds
- Other species of herd animals such as wilderbeasts
- Viruses and tumors in mammalian bodies – there is some limited evidence of coherent behavior in viruses and in groups of tumors within bodies.
- Vegetation – Some species of trees are known to grow with a fairly regular spacing to promote maximum growth. How species of vegetation "communicate" is an open question. One possible answer is through chemical signatures emitted in the soil by plant roots.
- Undersea Superorganisms

    The variety and characteristics of species in the oceans' depths is just beginning to be explored in detail. However superorganism-like behavior appears to be apparent in some familiar undersea species:

    - Coral Reefs
    - Dolphin Herds
    - Whale Herds

An even more exciting superorganism possibility that has recently surfaced[6] are massive carpets of large multi-cellular, spaghetti-like bacteria found in the depths of the Pacific Ocean off Peru and Chile. The area that is thickly covered (as much as one kilogram per square meter) by these bacteria is about 150,000 square kilometers (the area of Greece). These bacteria do not need oxygen. Instead they live on hydrogen sulphide in oxygen poor, deep waters. They are also found in similar waters off of the coasts of Panama, Ecuador, Namibia and Mexico.

While proof that these enormous masses of bacteria are superorganisms is not currently available the sulfur eating, deep ocean microbes described above suggest that these large bacteria may form superorganisms.

Thus the number of superorganism species is expanding significantly.

1.1.3 Perfect vs. Imperfect Superorganisms

The majority of social insects have hives or nests with absolute internal tranquility. There are one or more queens and a hierarchy of workers that work in concert to sustain and grow the nest or hive. Each individual performs her/his role perfectly with no internal dissension or deviation from the role assigned them by heredity. We call the nests/hives of these species of insects *perfect superorganisms* since they function as one perfectly healthy organism. The attine leafcutter ants are the leading example of perfect superorganisms. Their nests typically have millions of ants. They have a well-defined social hierarchy with many castes and function in perfect harmony – thus they are perfect superorganisms.[7]

There are other species of ants, notably some ponerine species, that have colonies in which internal conflicts occur such as duels for dominance including rebellions by low-ranking workers. Colonies of these types of ants are somewhat more like human societies where internal conflicts are not uncommon. We call ant colonies, which can have internal conflicts, *imperfect superorganisms*. They function as a unit but are capable of internal dissension. As noted earlier we believe human civilizations to be imperfect superorganisms.

1.1.3.1 An Imperfect Superorganism Example

Colonies of certain species of ants that have several queen ants[8] are excellent examples[9] of imperfect superorganisms. Each queen produces a group of follower worker arts. The worker

---

[6] Census of Marine Life (2010).
[7] Leafcutter ants have also made a major evolutionary advance by developing the ability to cut and use live plant material to feed their fungi gardens. Other ant species gather dead vegetation to use in feeding their fungi. By utilizing live plant material leafcutter ants have achieved a competitive advantage over other ant species. This capability is reflected in their large colonies and nests of great depth and extent – sometimes covering areas of up to 70 square meters or more with depths of over 4 meters.
[8] Rather like England in the time of Mary Queen of Scots and Elizabeth I.
[9] Holman, L., Proceedings of the Royal Society B, February 24, 2010.

ants produced by one queen may proceed to start killing the other queens until only their queen remains. The comparison to human civilizations in which civil wars take place is clear.

In the case of ants, however, sometimes a queen(s) will execute a survival strategy: the queen will produce fewer worker ants and thus retain more of her strength to fight off attacks by other queens' workers. This strategy works in some cases. But a counterstrategy can be used by the other queens' workers. They can detect by scent a queen that has held back on the production of workers, and the other queens' workers can selectively concentrate on killing the clever queen that retained strength by not producing workers. Clearly, Nature can execute Machiavellian strategies in imperfect superorganisms as Man can in civilizations!

Superorganism	Civilization
Cells	Individuals
Organs	Occupations
Sexual Organs	Fertile couples
Immune System	Guard stations, police & soldiers
Autoimmune and similar diseases	Conflicts between individuals & groups for dominance
Somatic Organs	Workers
Circulatory System	Food, materials, and Information distribution systems
Senses	Frontier and internal military posts & their communications network
Nervous System	Communications between the civilization's members
Body (skin & skeleton)	The civilization's territory
Individual Growth & Development	The growth of the civilization

Table 1.2. Comparison of a civilization with a superorganism.

1.1.3.2 Civilizations as Imperfect Superorganisms

Civilizations have often been latently thought of, and described, as persons since they are "born", they grow, they decay, and they "die." This personification of civilizations has often been criticized as simplistic.

We believe civilizations are best characterized as imperfect superorganisms. Table 1.2 compares features of civilizations with the features of an organism and reveals a close analogy. The following chapters of this book show that the same energetic/thermodynamic models of organism and superorganism growth also describe civilizations. Thus we also have quantitative grounds for identifying civilizations as superorganisms and calling them *SuperCivilizations*.

1.2 Energetic Principles For the Evolution of Superorganisms and Supercivilizations

The energetic principles at the basis of civilizational dynamics that we described in Blaha (2010) are:

If we treat civilizations as superorganisms we can develop a model of the growth of civilizations based on their ability to transform resources from the environment (both natural and human[10]) into internal growth. The reproductive power model of Brown et al[11] furnishes a natural starting point for the development of our growth model of civilizations viewed as superorganisms.[12] The purpose of the model of Brown et al was to consider the fitness of organisms in energetic terms of their ability to acquire energy[13] (resources) from their environment and to transform them into a form suitable to maintain their homeostasis and to grow (reproduce). Brown et al proposed the process:

> Rate of resource acquisition for reproduction →
> Capacity to transform Energy to reproductive work (energetics)

providing a relationship between fitness for survival, and energetics and thermodynamics.[14]

We take the basic general concept of their energy-based model and apply it to civilizations. We assume the rate at which a civilization grows is the result of two limiting processes: *the rate of resource acquisition* and *the rate of conversion of acquired resources into*

---

[10] Such as by conquest of rich neighboring civilizations or societies.
[11] Brown, J. H., Marquet, P. A., and Taper, M. L., The American Naturalist **142**, 573 (1993) developed their model for populations and genotypes. Unlike Brown et al who only examined the ultimate limiting solution we solved the dynamical equations that follow for all time to show the complete growth evolution of a superorganism.
[12] Other papers of relevance for studies of the growth and size of organisms and superorganisms include "Energetic Basis of Colonial Living in Social Insects" by Hou, C., Kaspart, M., Vander Zanden, H. B., and Gillooly, J. F., Proc. Nat. Acad. Sciences (2010); Moses, M. E. et al, The American Naturalist **171** 632 (2008); Brown, J. H. et al, Ecology **85** 1771 (2004); Allen, A. A. and Gillooly, J. F., Oikos **116** 1073 (2007); Ernst, S. K. M. et al, Ecology Letters **6** 990 (2003) and references therein. I am grateful to Professor Gillooly for providing me with a copy of his (and colleagues) PNAS paper.
[13] For a civilization energy is some combination of agricultural land, water, metals such as gold or copper, rocks and jewels, a productive population, wood, energy resources such as coal and oil, and so on.
[14] The model of Brown et al is a variation on the OGM (Ontogenetic Growth Model). As noted by Moses et al, The American Naturalist **171**, 632 (2008), "The OGM is based on the premise that metabolic rate, which is the overall rate of energy use, fuels growth and development and that allocation of this metabolic energy between production of new biomass and maintenance of existing biomass is the dominant process controlling growth." Thus the models have a similar premise and similar dynamic equations.

internal growth. We will treat the rate as the result of two conceptual steps or transitions (similar to chemical reactions) that transform resources R into growth G:

$$R + C_0 \rightarrow C_1$$

and

$$C_1 \rightarrow G + C_0$$

where C_0 is the rate of change of the civilization before resource acquisition and C_1 is the rate of change of the civilization after resource acquisition. We will assume the rate of resource acquisition is saturated (i.e. the maximal acquisition of available resources).

With this framework for growth and evolution we developed the cyclic harmonic oscillator theory for civilizations in Blaha (2010) that we discovered from historical data as described in Blaha (2002a). *Thus we have a theory of civilizations founded on general physical theory that works.*

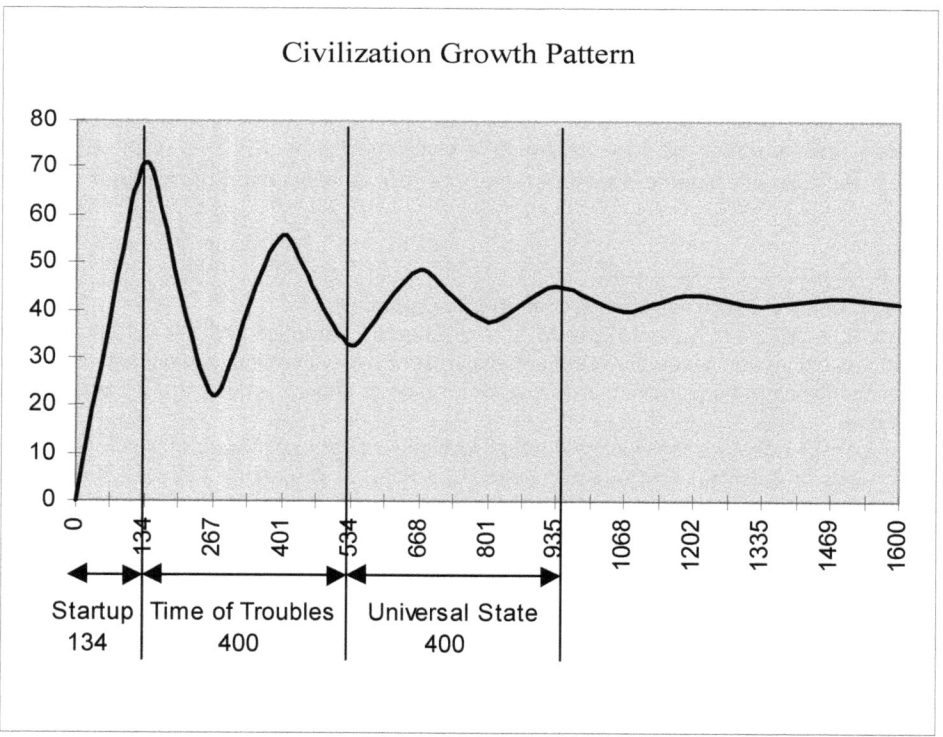

Figure 1.1. The standard growth pattern of a 1,000 year lifetime civilization plotted against time. The zero point of time marks the beginning of the civilization.

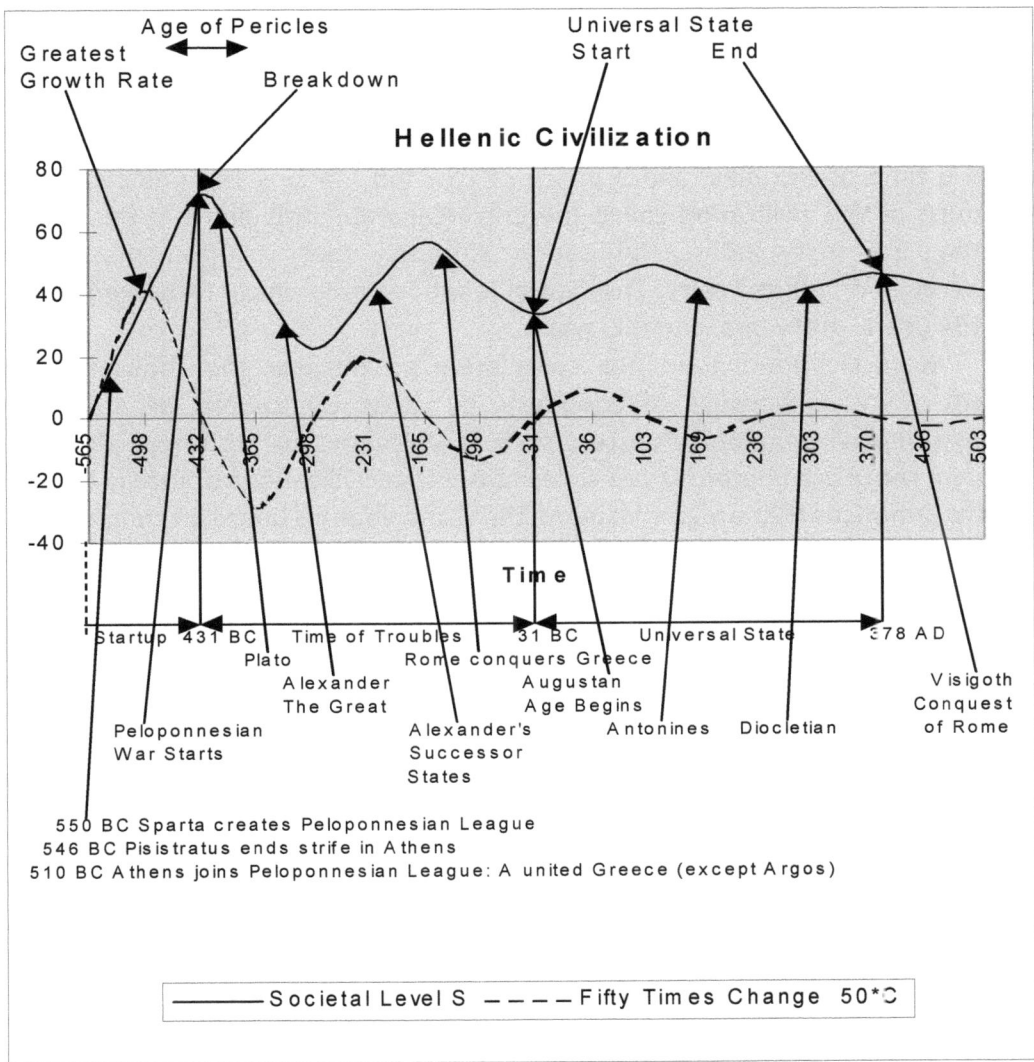

Figure 1.2. The pattern of Hellenic Civilization with key events marked to show how they follow the trends of ups and downs of the civilization's growth curve which we call the Societal level S. The change in S (its derivative) is plotted as the curve C multiplied by 50.

The general form of the ups and downs of a civilization is a cyclic pattern that declines with time since each subsequent "up" after a "down" has less available resources and/or ability to "energy" (resources) into new growth. Fig. 1.1 illustrates the declining cyclic pattern with time. There are usually three phases in the history of a civilization: the initial rapid startup phase, a downturn often called a time of troubles, and a phase of triumph marking the unification and greatness of the civilization called the universal state. This phase is based on a declining resource/resource utilization situation that is often masked by prosperity and political unity. The typical length of each phase is marked on Fig. 1.1: 134 years, 400 years, and 400 years.

Most civilizations do not completely go through the thousand year pattern of cycles because of conquests by other civilizations or nations or because of environmental disasters such as volcanoes or prolonged droughts. However there are numerous examples of isolated civilizations primarily in Africa and the Americas that do go through a thousand year lifetime and then expire – often for no apparent reason. Blaha (2010) thoroughly describes our theory and successfully applies it to over fifty civilizations throughout the world. Fig. 1.2 illustrates the pattern applied to the case of Hellenic civilization. Later we will see other examples illustrating the agreement of our theory with the history of civilizations.

1.3 Evolution based on the Energetics/Thermodynamics of Civilizations

From Blaha (2010):

> The evolution, or life history, of civilizations appears similar to the evolution of organisms and superorganisms. Progress has been made in the understanding of the evolution of organisms based on maximization of the fitness of the individuals in a population. Fitness has been identified as the rate that surplus resources can be extracted from an environment and devoted to reproduction or growth of a species, colony or superorganism. Surplus resources are defined to be resources beyond those necessary for maintenance or growth of an individual.
>
> Thus fitness is equated with reproduction or growth, which in turn is identified with the acquisition of surplus resources or energy.[15] Growth of an organism or superorganism then becomes a question of energetics or thermodynamics. This possibility was envisioned by

---

[15] For organisms see Brown, J. H., Marquet, P. A., and Taper, M. L., The American Naturalist **142**, 573 (1993); For superorganisms see Hou, C., Kaspart, M., Vander Zanden, H. B., and Gillooly, J. F., Proc. Nat. Acad. Sciences (2010).

Boltzmann in 1905 in a frequently cited remark: "[The] struggle for existence is a struggle for free energy available for work." And later by Lotka in 1922, "In the struggle for existence, the advantage must go to those organisms whose energy-capturing devices are most efficient in directing available energy into channels favorable to the preservation of the species."

Based on energetics/thermodynamics it is possible to develop a model for growth (reproduction/fitness) that appears to be successful for both organisms, and for superorganisms of insect colonies.

1.4 A Deterministic Theory of Civilizations Exists

In the previous sections we have summarized our macro-theory of civilizations and showed how it followed from fundamental energetic principles in a manner similar to other species. Blaha (2010) describes the mathematics of the theory in detail with discussions of many related topics such as the impact of technology, the environment, conflicts between civilizations, and the impact of the industrial revolution. It considers over 50 civilizations around the world and shows our theory successfully agrees with their histories. It also considers the pre-civilization period from 11,000 B.C. to 3,500 B.C.

The success of a theory is to account for known history, and to predict the future. Since the appearance of our first book in 2002 in which we made predictions for the 21st Century twelve years have elapsed. This is not a particularly long time interval but a comparison of the major events that have happened in these twelve years is in remarkable agreement with our predictions. We will show this in the next chapter. We will then consider what to expect in the remainder of the 21st Century. In short we see a situation reminiscent of the symbolic depiction of the book's cover: warfare and major water shortages associated with global warming – rather like the end of the Classical Mayan civilization.[16]

After the consideration of current times, we will examine new Peruvian, Pre-Mayan, Mayan, Anatolian, and Early Egyptian data that has appeared in the past two or three years that closely agrees with our prior predictions. *Given the close agreement with historical/archaeological data and its foundation in fundamental principles, we feel our rigorous macro-theory is correct.*

---

[16] There are of course major cultural and social differences. But there is an analogy in the political and environmental events.

1.5 Free Will and Our Rigorous Macro-Theory of Civilizations

Many students of History find it difficult to believe that the History of civilizations has a well-defined, mathematical form. There are so many factors that influence the history of civilizations that it seems almost inconceivable that a mathematics theory is possible. In addition the belief in free will, which most people have, further suggests a mathematical theory of civilizations is not possible.

Balanced against those considerations we simply offer the massive amount of historical data in Blaha (2010) that agrees well with our theory. Further we offer the new data presented in this book which also agrees with the theory.

Lastly, we point out that the theory is based on energetic principles (thermodynamics) that apply to all social species and also species that form colonies such as bacterial colonies. The theory is thus not simply a phenomenology, although it began that way in 2002, but truly a theory based on fundamental principles.

Given this strong evidence for our theory one may ask: If Man's macro-history for the past 6,000 years is largely determined by our rigorous mathematical theory then is Man doomed to follow historical cycles no matter what efforts are made to have an advancing, set of civilizations such as suggested on the back cover of this book and Blaha (2002a). Can Man advance based on the informed decisions of Man's leaders and peoples? We feel that the small-scale events of history are determined by individual decisions but the concatenation of these events into macro-history trends will conform to our theory because of the theory's basis in thermodynamics (statistics). We have free will on an individual basis but group behavior on a large scale is statistical and thus determined.

New Support for a Superorganism Macro-Theory of Civilizations from Current World Trends

2. The Agreement Between Our Supercivilization Theory and Current Trends

In this chapter we will compare the predictions of our book, *The Rhythms of History*,[17] for current major civilizations with the events that have happened in the 12 years since then and emerging trends. Although this time period is short, reasonably convincing evidence will become apparent that our theory has been successful in anticipating major civilization history since our first book in 2002.

Our subsequent books make the same predictions.

2.1 Our Theory's Predictions in Blaha (2002a)

In this section we will simply reproduce the predictions in chapter 9 of Blaha (2002a):[18,19]

9. Implications for the Future of Civilizations

The Immediate Future of Current Civilizations

The theory we have developed enables us to make some general predictions about the near term prospects of current civilizations. These observations are subject to change due to chance historical events, environmental effects such as global warming or major volcanic eruptions, events such as plagues and epidemics, and the appearance of singular individuals such as a Napoleon who might have a temporary but major impact on history. Despite these possibilities the overall pattern of political and economic

---

[17] Blaha (2002a)

[18] In this section we have introduced the name "Technic" for Western civilization and the postfix "technic" for other civilizations in Fig. 31 below. In 2002 we realized that the technological revolution – primarily in communications and thus social intercourse – would have a profound influence on world societies and culture. Since then the impact of the Internet, and portable communications and computational devices, has truly transformed world civilizations.

[19] We will indicate trends and situations since 2002 supporting our theory with **bold type** in this section of chapter 9 of Blaha (2002a).

events that represent parts of long-term trends are embodied in the predictions of the general theory.

We will first look at the present state, and near term prospects, of individual civilizations. Then we will examine the combined effect of these prospects on the future.

The next figure shows the current phases of some major contemporary civilizations: the startup phase, the breakdown, and the "rout" phase after the breakdowns based on the following data.[20]

	Technic	JapoTechnic	RussoTechnic	SinoTechnic	IndoTechnic	PetroIslamic
Startup	1780	1868	1917	1950	1950	1950
Breakdown	1914	2002	2051	2084	2084	2084
Rout End	2048	2136	2185	2218	2218	2218

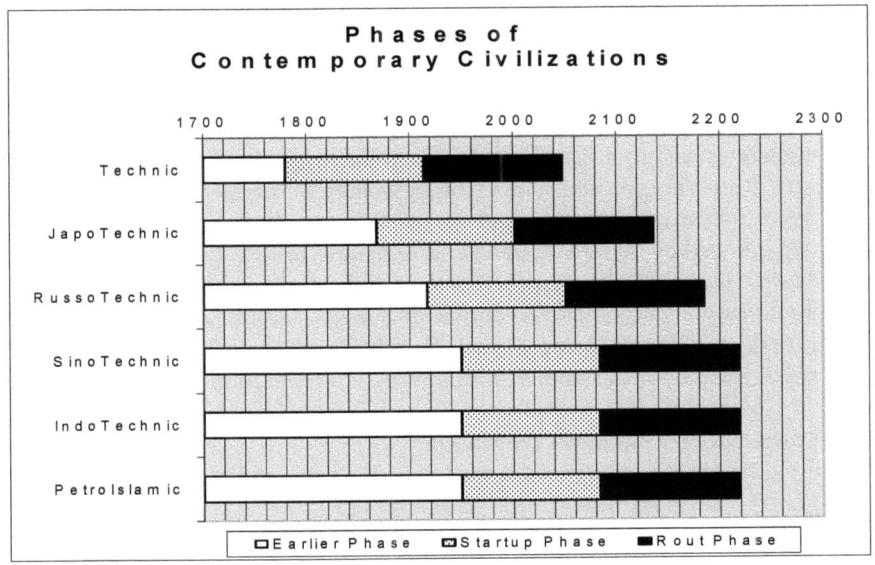

Figure 31. A comparison of the phases of contemporary civilizations. The "earlier" phase is simply part of the period of a predecessor civilization before a startup begins. The predecessor may be similar to its successor.

---

[20] The terminology used here was used by Arnold Toynbee in his opus on world civilizations. The phases are shown in Fig. 1.1. The startup phase of 134 years is the phase of initial rapid growth in a civilization. The "breakdown" is the point where the rapid growth breaks down, and a downturn period called a "rout" occurs which lasts for about 400 years.

Western Technological (Technic) Civilization

Technic civilization appears to have had a startup in approximately 1780. The rapid industrialization of the western world and the growth of democratic ideas both occurred during the 134 years that followed. An apparent side effect of both of these trends was the development of the concept of the total war of populations that started with the breakdown in 1914 of the peace of Europe. Before that war Europe was more or less at peace and citizens of the leading countries enjoyed an international culture and a belief in a developing universal peace. World War I shattered that hope and began a time of troubles that contains both world wars as well as the Cold War with its threat of massive nuclear destruction that lasted until roughly 1990.

Writing in the year 2002 we see a new threat of nuclear destruction from nuclear proliferation to secondary powers and, potentially, to well-financed terrorists.

The period from 1914 to 2048 represents a "rout" within a time of troubles. A "rally" is projected to begin in 2048. What do these phases represent? The rout reflects a decline in the overall "spirit" of Western civilization. Since 1914 the western world, and particularly Europe, has seen the disappearance of vast empires created in the Third World: Asia, Africa and South America. **The attitudes of Western civilization have also changed from a feeling of cultural and political superiority to a sense of equality and, perhaps, due to the cultural and immigration invasion from former colonies, and subject states,** to a feeling of disadvantage in certain areas such as philosophy and the arts. This decline, which may be a welcome change towards an egalitarian world, nevertheless represents a rout for Western civilization. The population declines being experienced by many European countries also reflect this "spiritual" decline. People are having fewer children partly because they realize that their economic horizons are limited and having children represents a major expense. The rout in Western civilization is predicted to end in approximately 2048. Then a rally is predicted for 134 years with a corresponding revival in the spirit of Western civilization.

Contemporary Japanese Civilization

Japan experienced a startup in 1868 due to the opening of Japan by the United States. The shock of western technology led Japan to totally reorganize itself to meet a new future. This reorganization was depicted internally as a restoration of ancient Japanese values and called the Meiji Restoration.

Japan rapidly progressed during this growth phase. Japanese literacy progressed from near zero to one hundred per cent literacy in little more than one generation. Japanese industrial and military progress led to the defeat of a major European power Russia in the Russo-Japanese War of 1904-5.

Despite a complete defeat and occupation in World War II Japan resumed impressive growth afterwards that led to its position as the second largest economy in the world by the late 1980's.

The events since 1868 happened within an extraordinary growth period that is scheduled to end in roughly 2002 according to our theory. Interestingly, Japan has been experiencing difficulties in this last generation of four generations of growth.

Starting around 1988 Japan has experienced increasing economic difficulties. In addition Japan is starting to experience social difficulties associated with a rapidly aging population and low birth rate. **As of this writing (March, 2002) it appears that Japan must undertake major financial reforms in order to restore its economy.** Under present conditions Japan's economy is expected to contract by over four per cent in the next year by financial analysts. The financial reforms necessary to make Japan's economy healthy again will undoubtedly cause serious economic dislocations. The effects of these reforms may initiate the breakdown projected by our theory. Afterwards Japan is projected to enter into a time of troubles lasting four hundred years.

Contemporary Chinese Civilization

China was unified for the first time since the Manchu Dynasty in 1949 with the complete takeover of mainland China by the Communists. The Communists embarked on a program of education and economic and industrial development that led to a Chinese nuclear bomb in 1964 and a Chinese space program in 2000. The rapid development of China as an industrial power and as a technological power—particularly in the 1990's, and its unification of the majority of the Chinese people suggest that 1950 be taken as the point of a startup of 134 years of growth that may be expected to continue until roughly 2084 when a breakdown is projected to occur. We will identify 1950 as the beginning of a technological society based on Chinese culture that we will call SinoTechnic civilization.

At the time of this writing in March, 2002 China is experiencing growth pains in the form of financial problems. **Our analysis suggests that China will emerge from these issues and continue strong growth until 2084** when it will enter a time of troubles.

Contemporary Indian Civilization

India received independence from Great Britain in 1950. Since receiving independence India has made great strides in technology and industry including the development of a sizable computer industry, the development of nuclear energy including a nuclear bomb and the development of rocket technology. Despite an enormous population increase modern India has made great strides in its standard of living for the westernized component of its population. Based on this recent history, and especially in comparison to the preceding hundred years, **it appears that India is in a major growth phase that we will take to have begun in 1950.**

If the growth startup did indeed begin in 1950, then a breakdown can be expected in roughly 2084 when India will enter a time of troubles. **The new Indian civilization of over a billion people combines technology and Indian culture.** We call this civilization IndoTechnic.

The cause of the anticipated breakdown can only be conjectured at this time. But it may well be the result of a conflict between traditional Indian society of which the vast majority of Indians are members and modern, technological India consisting of a hundred million or so individuals. The breakdown may be similar to the Iranian revolution of the 1980's which was a reaction of traditional Islamic culture to rapid modernization.

Contemporary Arab Islamic Civilization

The Arab Islamic civilization of the last 800 years is projected to end in approximately 2172. If so, then an interregnum or new startup is possible at that time.

It is possible that a startup has already occurred due to the oil wealth of the Arabs, the end of western colonial dominance and the creation of Israel in a major religious center of Islam. It seems reasonable to date the beginning of this probable startup at roughly 1950 based on these factors.

Since 1950 there has been a massive infusion of technology into the Middle East purchased with Arab oil wealth that has led to industrial growth, atomic power, and scientific and engineering prowess. **This growth phase raises the question whether a new civilization has started in this region – a new civilization grounded in Islam but committed to technological progress.** Since the basis for this growth is petroleum resources it seems reasonable to call this proposed new civilization the PetroIslamic civilization.

The growth phase of PetroIslamic civilization (if it indeed has started) is projected to end in 2084 according to our theory. The growth phase will be followed by a time of troubles lasting four hundred years. After the time of troubles the creation of an Islamic universal state is projected realizing the dreams of the Pan Islamic Movement.

Contemporary Russian Civilization

The Russian branch of Orthodox Christian civilization ended in 1881. In 1917 the Russian Revolution began a phase of rapid industrialization. Ultimately this led to brilliant Russian technical achievements in science and in space. While the empire that the USSR built has been disbanded, **Russia remains an empire in terms of its geographical size and in terms of its military capabilities.**

The **enormous growth of Russia since 1917** raises the question whether it entered a startup phase for the development of a technically based civilization within the Russian cultural experience. The question is one that cannot be answered definitively for at least several hundred years. We will provisionally assume Russian civilization did undergo a startup in 1917 and call that civilization RussoTechnic civilization. If so, the growth phase should end in a breakdown around 2051.

The Mix of Contemporary Civilizations 2002

An observer of the international scene in 2002 sees a new interplay of civilizations taking place. The United States and other nations of Western civilization have shifted from the relative complacency of the 1990's when war appeared to be a thing of the past to an open-ended war on terrorism. In the last twenty years of the twentieth century Western civilization developed a largely peaceful relationship with other important civilizations on earth with the exception of Islamic civilization. Islamic civilization has been engaged in a covert expansionism that is evidenced by conflicts in Nigeria, the Philippines, Indonesia, and the Sudan among others. The Saudi government sponsors this expansionism through an extensive program of mosque building, education and other forms of support in the western world, particularly in the United States. Islam has an active grass roots program with a goal of converting the world to Islam.

The peoples of Islam are generally poor and part of Third World poverty. They see the West, and particularly the United States, as engaged in a conspiracy to prevent them from emerging from poverty.

Most importantly, they see the West as the main support of Israel. In the Islamic view Israel is an occupier of sacred Islamic ground that was won by conquest. In view of the inability of Islamic governments to win a conventional war with Israel, elements within the Islamic peoples have formed terrorist groups to fight Israel and it greatest supporter the United States. While the United States was basking in the afterglow of its successful war with Iraq, terrorist groups were training and preparing for a widened terrorist offensive against their perceived enemies. The events of September 11, 2001 are one of the results of their worldwide preparations.

The response of the United States to September 11th was an attack on the al Qaeda terrorist organization and their Afghan Taliban allies. This attack was widely viewed in the Islamic world as part of a war between Western civilization and Islamic civilization. The West tried to portray this conflict as a war on terrorism.

The analysis that we have presented shows the West to be in the latter stages of a decline of societal level. On the other hand Islamic civilization may well be in a growth phase. Certainly its oil resources which are of vital importance for the economy of the West give Islam a major card to play against western military strength.

A historical perspective suggests the terrorist activities correspond to barbarian attacks on a civilization. Barbarian attacks are a familiar part of the history of civilizations. **The immigration of large numbers of Muslims to western countries** is similar to the migration of barbarians into the Roman Empire in the latter days of the empire. These analogies, and the crucial role of the great oil wealth of the Islamic world for the Western industrial democracies, would appear to be a bad portent for the future. It must be remembered that the terrorist leadership of al Qaeda came from the affluent Arab community—not from poor Arabs. It came from Arabs who were most acquainted with the West.

However there is an important difference between the Islamic-Western situation and the Roman-barbarian conflicts. The barbarians only became a serious threat to Rome towards the end of western Hellenic civilization. Today it appears that

Western civilization is barely past a new beginning that started in 1780. The societal level of Western civilization gives it the internal strength to turn back the attacks of barbarians into the foreseeable future. Later in the twenty first century when western Technic civilization begins a rally and Islamic civilization perhaps enters a time of troubles the West should enjoy an even stronger position.

Another important current situation is the continuing Japanese financial crisis. By our analysis Japanese civilization is nearing the end of its growth phase and approaching a breakdown. If this analysis is correct and Japan does have a catastrophic event, the effect on the world's financial condition could be profound. Therefore the West should make a major effort to ease the Japanese through its financial difficulties.

China is still in the midst of the growth phase of SinoTechnic civilization that should last until a breakdown that is projected to occur in 2083. **China is aggressively moving forward in science and technology with a major space program, and major scientific programs including the development of a larger nuclear arsenal.** China is also trying to instill bravery and courage in its children as part of their educational programs. Further China is promoting economic development and the exploitation of natural resources at the maximum possible rates. It is particularly trying to exploit less developed regions such as western China and developing a major presence along its Siberian border with Russia. These trends suggest China may attempt to press its claims for parts of Siberia if Russia should become weaker.

Russia experienced a major dip in its development in the 1990's due to its changeover to a capitalist economy. **Russia appears to be beginning to move forward. Its massive natural resources and agricultural potential give it a great potential for further growth.** Its growth phase is projected to end in about fifty years (2051) with a breakdown. Global warming may act to benefit Russia agriculturally, and in the development of Siberia. Russia has the potential to exploit the growth phase for maximum benefit. An improved economy and health care system could lead to an increase in Russian population growth. A democratic, vibrant Russia could also expect immigration from Germany and other parts of Western Europe as well as the Third World. With a resurgent China eyeing Siberia, Russia can be expected to continue good relations with the West.

India has made great strides in development in the 1980's and 1990's particularly in the computer industry. **Having created a dynamic technology sector IndoTechnic civilization is enjoying a major growth phase.** A breakdown in growth is projected for 2084. The nature of this breakdown is societal. It could be the result of a major conflict between the westernized technologically oriented Indian sub-society and the Hindu fundamentalist sub-society that has emerged in recent years.

India is clearly trying to establish itself as a major world power. It has a continuing conflict with Pakistan that will result in a de facto concession by Pakistan that India is the overwhelmingly dominant power on the Indian subcontinent. The latent conflict with China in common border regions will likely result in a continuing stalemate.

The Mix of Contemporary Civilizations 2050

An observer of the international scene in 2050 will see a much changed world. Not only will the effects of global warming be very evident, but there may be major changes in the status of the various civilizations.

Russia, China, India and the Islamic world will have enjoyed major growth phases bringing them all to new levels of prosperity as civilizations. In such a situation one can expect that there will be temptations for all parties to exploit their strength and prosperity by aggressive activities economically, politically, or in space. Russia, China and India all have major space programs. The next fifty years are likely to be more or less peaceful (in the sense that there will not be a world war) due to the overwhelming strength of the United States.

The growth of these countries in a general atmosphere of peace, and the drain on the United States in its role as a world leader, will lead the world to a situation reminiscent of Europe before World War I.

Rather than being a great hope for the future, widespread affluence may actually promote conflict and war.

The Mix of Contemporary Civilizations 2100

An observer of the international scene in 2100 may see a much changed world from 2050. With all major civilizations having undergone a breakdown in the previous century, all civilizations will be simultaneously in a time of troubles. It is natural to think that this confluence of phases cannot be a happy portent. While the breakdowns are individual according to our theory since they stem from the social nature of mankind, a confluence of routs would seem to lead to a period of turmoil.

2.2 Overall Civilizational Trends and Events Consistent with Our Theory

Section 2.1 describes predictions of our theory for major contemporary world civilizations. In this section we will list the significant trends and events in the history of major civilizations in the past twelve years that agree with our analysis.

Technic (Western)

In decline with a decreasing native population; Increasing immigration from Africa, Asia and the Americas south of the United States; Decreasing financial power represented by increasing debt; Increasing social problems. Overall status in decline.

Russian

Growing with a major increase in military strength (modernized army, air force and growing navy); Expansionist as witnessed by Georgian and Ukrainian adventurism as well as expanded claims to much of the mineral rich Arctic and pressure in Central Asia such as Kazakhstan; Increasing financial strength built largely on oil and natural gas exports; Major space initiatives such as a massive new rocket capable of flying a manned spaceship to Mars.

China

Growing military strength (first aircraft carrier, modernized army and air force) based on major growth in industry and financial strength; Expansionist moves into Central Asia through political means and expansion/assertion of claims to the East China Sea; Increasing dominance of the computer and high tech hardware industry to the point that the US military relies on China for parts; Growing space program with plans for manned moon landing and other ambitious ventures.

India

Growing high tech computer software and support industry; Expanding industrial strength; A growing space program with ambitious goals; Improving social situation.

Japan

Stagnant financial sector; Low growth in major export industries; Increasing competition from China and South Korea; Conflicts with China and North Korea; Aging population creating social and financial problems.

Islamic

Growing military and financial strength in Iran, Gulf States and Saudi Arabia; Turmoil in Afghanistan, North Africa, the Middle East, and Iraq with the overthrow of dictators and civil wars; The turmoil could lead to a unifying countermovement and the creation of a true Islamic Nation; The appearance of a Mahdi (Islamic messiah) to lead a unifying jihad would result in the creation of a powerful state. Islam continues to expand throughout Africa, and in Europe and the US through emigration – a peaceful process that may have major political and military implications. Islam, a religion with a strong political character, is growing in a major way.

As this book is nearing completion (August 25, 2014) a remarkable group has emerged – ISIS (Islamic State in Iraq and Syria) in Iraq and Syria with a strong leader (Abu Bakr al Baghdadi) that is sweeping through these countries in a manner reminiscent of Muhammad's early conquests in the 7th century. While the United States is making a limited air war effort together with supplying weaponry to the Kurds and other ISIS opponents, the ISIS surge has the potential to create a unified Islamic nation of Sunni Muslims ranging from Iraq to southern Africa that would be the counterpart of Shia Iran. While ISIS may not succeed, its success reflects the potential of Islam for unification and jihad, if not through ISIS, then through a future movement.

2.3 Are there any Points of Disagreement?

It is quite clear from the previous section and our prior books that the situation of current major civilizations is consistent with our theory – published in 2002.

3. Major Hazards Facing the World Today

In the previous chapter we described the trends in major world civilizations and showed that they agreed with the predictions of our theory of civilizations first published in 2002. This chapter describes major potential problems that could strongly affect world civilizations and perhaps even cause the end of some of them. Based on the history of past civilizations we believe most of these problems will be successfully dealt with through adaptation and the development of new solutions. The following chapter on the state of world civilizations in 3000 AD is based on this assumption.

3.1 Major World Epidemic Causing the Death of 25% -70% of Humanity

The recent local "short term" epidemics that have appeared in the past decade have raised the possibility of a major plague similar to the Black Death of the 1600's. In particular, the current spread of Ebola in Africa, and its increasing range that might bring it to other parts of the world in a global pandemic, has pointedly raised this issue. We can hope that this particular disease will be eradicated or contained.

But it brings up a fact that must be faced by an increasingly populous humanity: *the more crowded that earth becomes, the more likely that new or changed viruses will develop.* Humans furnish a habitat for the growth and differentiation of viruses and bacteria. Population growth which will bring us to a world population of about nine billion by mid-21st century will lead to an ever increasing likelihood of lethal epidemics. One might view this phenomenon as Nature attempting to offset the growth of a species (us) by introducing mechanisms to lower the growth rate, or even to lower the population of the species: Nature attempts to establish/maintain equilibrium.

Consequently, the onset of new potential epidemics will continue. The dispersal of people due to travel and migration will facilitate the spread of diseases. Air travel is a particularly effective mechanism to rapidly spread disease.

If a global pandemic occurs the populations of the major civilizations will be severely reduced. The conveniences afforded populations: food, water, economic activity, technological progress, and so on would be strongly affected and perhaps ended for a period of decades if not centuries. Civilizations would then have to begin anew with the surviving remnants of their populations.

3.2 A Major Nuclear War

In 1990 the collapse of the Soviet Union led most people to believe that large wars, particularly nuclear wars, would not occur. A universal peace, admittedly with hot spots such as the Middle East, Iraq and Iran, would ensue. In the 1990's it did appear that a new era of world peace was developing. The situation was reminiscent of the harmony of Europe in the late 19th century when an international society existed. The harmony was broken by national conflicts that developed in the first decade of the 20th century that blossomed into the First World War.[21]

It became clear in 2001 that wars, even large wars, would be possible. The attack on the World Trade Center in New York signaled the major dissatisfaction of a sizeable segment of the Islamic civilization population with Western civilization. This dissatisfaction has blossomed to an ongoing terrorist war between Muslim factions and Western nations in particular. The mini-wars in Iraq and Afghanistan are concrete examples of this continuing struggle.

Recently we have seen the Russians, enjoying their new prosperity, revive their military potential and start an expansion into former Soviet territories such as Georgia and now eastern Ukraine. One can only wonder if White Russia and Kazakhstan may be the next victims. It appears that Russian civilization is in the growth mode predicted by our theory. Further evidence can be seen in their ambitious space program which includes nuclear rockets and ultra-large

---

[21] Interestingly the relative peace of the 1990's is now being broken by Islamic, Russian, and Chinese expansionism. Whether history is repeating itself is problematic. But the current relative peace is fragile and a war perhaps instigated by Russia (with the tacit acquiescence of China) is becoming more likely. It is surprising that the Russian-Chinese border disputes have disappeared, or been "put under the table", in the past few years suggesting a partnership in expansionism in other regions.

conventional rockets. These rockets have the potential for manned flights to Mars and perhaps the asteroid belt which has sizeable planetoids potentially rich in valuable metals.

The Chinese have also entered into an expansionist phase as part as our predicted growth period. In addition to expanding in computer hardware they will probably create a jet industry to compete with Boeing, and will succeed because of the labor intensive character of this industry and the low pay of Chinese workers. They have started to expand their territorial claims by asserting their ownership of a large part of the East China Sea in competition with Japan, the Philippines, and Vietnam. They are also financing pro-Chinese political parties in Central Asia. In both these regions China is seeking access to major oil suppliers.

Japan is rearming with the creation of its first mini-aircraft carrier and is vigorously disputing China's claims in the East China Sea. Its military is not capable of a war with China. Japan lies under the US umbrella for its security.

Islam is in a state of disarray with many of the dictators of its various countries deposed and replaced with fragile democracies. Unless a Mahdi (messiah) appears who will unify the "Islamic Nation" it will continue to grow economically but remain politically weak. Its major forces for war are terrorist groups and Iran.

The United States wishes for peace and is making efforts around the world to prevent wars. However its citizenry is opposed to wars where American ground troops are engaged. Russia, China and Islam are well aware of this sentiment for peace and are obviously taking advantage of it by pursuing their expansionist efforts.

What has this overview of the current situation to do with nuclear war? The presence of these conflicts, and potentially greater conflicts, as well as nuclear proliferation to Iran and North Korea in particular and to Pakistan, India Israel, and Egypt, opens the possibility of nuclear war. For many years nuclear war was regarded as unthinkable (except perhaps from the 1950's up to the Cuban Missile Crisis). Now with a variety of players with nuclear weaponry, the stage is set for mini nuclear wars at first followed by major nuclear wars. It is well to remember that guns were first viewed as horrors when they appeared in the 1300's. Then slowly they became more widely used. By the 1500's they were standard equipment for European armies and also being used in Asia and Japan.

The horror of guns initially felt had disappeared after a century or so. Today we see the beginning of a similar scenario with frequent threats by Iran to "nuke" Israel and by North Korea to "nuke" South Korea, and, further, to "nuke" the US White House. Talk is often a predecessor of action. Talk of mini nuclear wars is now prevalent. The possibility of these wars, if they happen, will ease the acceptability of major nuclear wars subsequently.

A major nuclear war will have an enormous impact on all contemporary civilizations either directly or indirectly through nuclear fallout or a "nuclear winter" putting enough dust in the air to cause a global cold spell and major crop failures. And there would be no great power to help rebuild the world as the United States did after World War II. Consequently the rebuilding process would be lengthy – of the order of perhaps centuries – and the privation horrible. Further details of the collapse of world civilizations in this case need not be described to the reader.

3.3 Civil Unrest, Corruption and Violence

The period of relative international calm since the end of the Cold War in 1990 started as a time of rejoicing over the apparent end of the threat of major nuclear war. However the downturn in the United States and other Western economies, and the period of peace, has led to civil unrest, and increasing corruption and violence. The times are very difficult for the average family – meeting ends from lower paying jobs and from government unemployment and social security payments, has put enormous financial pressure on the middle classes and led to a large scale breakdown in families. Teen age children are being exited from their families due to lack of income. They are homeless; they turn to crime and drugs. They become embedded in a subculture of violence and degradation.

Crime rates seem to be declining in many areas. But they are declining because of the massive amount of unreported crime and corruption that reach into business, government, and law enforcement.

The United States is clearly becoming a divided class conscious country. The "haves" have jobs/income that support them well. The "have-nots" have inadequate income and turn to crime in increasing numbers burglaries, shoplifting, extortion, and so on. The "have-nots" are well aware that their prospects are poor – as are the prospects of their children. Unlike the Great Depression when the poor were generally accepting of their lot, today's "have-nots" are angry and are increasingly showing it in everyday life, in gang involvement, and in increased crime.

The situation in the United Kingdom and in Western Europe is similar but not yet as pronounced as in the United States, to which recent large scale hard times are new. But those countries are also moving in the direction of civil unrest and increasing crime and violence.

Other countries are also experiencing civil unrest for a variety of reasons. In many cases the unrest is tied to rises in the price or availability of food, and rises in the price of other basics such as transportation costs. Brazil is an example of this phenomenon in 2013. There are cases of unrest in other countries as well.

The media have a hand in increasing the tendency towards crime, violence and degradation. The news media focus on it – the gorier the better for their ratings. The movie and television entertainment media realize that sex and violence sell. So they give the public "what they want." This creates a feedback loop – crime, sex, and violence beget crime, sex, and violence.

The impact on Western Civilization of the picture that we have sketched above is clear: the downturn predicted by our theory is happening and it is very visible in the popular culture, and the behavior, of Western civilization. This social decline is a major art of the decline of Western (Technic) civilization. The decline is masked by massive government spending and by increasing technology. It is also masked by an increasing tolerance of previously unacceptable behavior. The possible consequences of this social breakdown range from political chaos as represented somewhat by the Tea Party faction to a private little civil war between the haves and have-nots in everyday life that diminishes the strength of the country and the quality and happiness of everyday life. The possibility of the development of sizeable extremist parties such as appeared in Germany in the 1920's is not excluded. The value of the dollar is declining significantly just as the German mark declined in the 1920's although the dollar decline is much less sharp than the mark's decline in that period.

We conclude that Western (Technic) civilization is experiencing a social decline as predicted by our theory that should bottom around 2048. (See Fig. 31 in chapter 2.) This decline if accentuated by conflicts with Russia or China could result in a major collapse of Western civilization. In this case these other civilizations might well collapse as well.

3.4 Financial Collapse

A world-wide financial collapse is a possibility given the current international financial situation. The US and other Western nations are all deeply in debt with the exception of Germany which has avoided debt at the price of higher unemployment and slower economic progress.

If a financial collapse occurs in Western civilization then China would collapse as well since the US is by far its major market. India would also be significantly affected. Russia alone would not be severely affected except for its European oil exports. It could circumvent this problem through barter transactions with Western Europe.

3.5 Environmental Deterioration

The world is going through a process of global warming which will benefit some countries but will cause problems for the majority of countries. Due to the relative slowness of global warming most countries will be able to undertake measures to alleviate global warming problems. Some countries such as Bangladesh will be mostly submerged as ocean levels rise. Given sufficient aid it could build hills and dikes to stem the rise in water levels in part. It would then become a country of islands and canals.

Global warming and rising ocean levels are much talked about aspects of environmental deterioration. But the more important issue is the massive rise in the amount of waste from the population and industry. Approximately one quarter of the earth's arable land has been severely polluted by waste. The ocean is polluted by toxic metals such as mercury, and by massive amounts of garbage (especially plastic materials) that are starting to form islands.

The ocean has been the main dumping grounds for waste based on the notion that dilution eliminates the toxic hazards of waste. This is no longer true. Ocean pollution has reached the point where the fishing industry will become unable to supply non-toxic fish. It is little realized that fish is a major part of the diet of many countries.

We conclude that continuing current waste disposal policies coupled with the projected major increase in world population will lead to a polluted world with a much lower quality of life, much higher levels of birth defects in children, and a future decline in all major world civilizations.

3.6 Tectonic or Asteroid Disasters

Major volcanic eruptions such as Krakatoa could cause major disasters in all the world's civilizations primarily by reducing agricultural production and increasing health problems.

A major asteroid impact could destroy all civilizations if sufficiently large. It would create dust in the atmosphere, block the sun, and destroy plant and animal life.

4. 3000 AD Based on the Trend of World Civilizations

To predict the future in these uncertain times is a hazardous occupation. To predict one day in advance is difficult. To predict one thousand years in advance is perhaps foolhardy. In this chapter we will attempt to predict the state of world civilizations in 3000 AD based on our theory of civilizations, the nature of Man, the current megatrends in world civilizations, and the change in civilizations in the past one thousand years. In so predicting we will assume that there have been no major catastrophes of the sort envisioned in the previous chapter.

We will also assume that Man has not created a major civilization in space or on other planets and planetoids, and that no contact of a significant nature has occurred with alien civilizations.

4.1 Social Nature of the Earth's Population in 3000 AD

The people of earth will undoubtedly be different in 3000 AD Our only guide to the nature of the difference is the change in the social nature of Man in the past 1,000 years from 1,000 AD to the present. Generally the personal characteristics of Man have changed in a number of ways. We can summarize the changes in a list which describes the major changes:

1. People have become kinder in general and less given to cruelty. Torture, vicious treatment, and games embodying deadly conflicts have diminished substantially. Warfare however has not changed for the better. One thousand years ago farmers and other non-combatants were not generally slaughtered since the victors would benefit from the survival of these groups. In the past century non-combatants have been slaughtered frequently in Asian, European and recent African wars as

well. The appearance of terrorists as a force devoted to the slaughter of innocent people is also a relatively new feature of the past two centuries.[22] Based on these observations it appears that there will be a general growth in individual gentility as 3000 AD is approached. But if there are wars and conflicts the brutality of the past will continue and may be greater due to technology: atomic attacks and improved high tech warfare. One can only hope that people will realize that the world would be a happy place if people would just act like human beings.

2. The nature of society has changed due to vastly improved communications technology. As a result much of the world has developed a knowledge of world conditions. On the positive side: the general educational level of people has risen; people have developed democratic viewpoints; it is much harder for dictators to suppress their peoples; and travel, trade and emigration have increased. On the negative side: communications media have many times increased tensions between nations and groups; individual privacy has been significantly diminished; the Big Brother climate of government and factional snooping has increased throughout the world; nations, religions and special interest groups have developed a greater awareness of differences with others often promoting increased hostility – not understanding; and the deluge of information from the news media with its focus on tragedies, sordid events, and conflicts can only be viewed as dispiriting. In 3000 we can only expect more advanced communication capabilities which would seem to favor the negative aspects listed above. In addition the tendency to communicate through devices rather than face to face is increasing and may well cause a lowering of direct social intercourse by people – less sociability and more distancing of people. This change may lead to a greater divergence of opinions – a more fractured society.

3. Today we have large movements of population taking place through emigration. The major recipient of emigration is the United States

---

[22] Terrorists were frequently called rebels in the past. But their tactics were not dissimilar to the terrorists of today: the slaughter of opponents without regard to their combatant status.

because of its relative prosperity. In 3000 AD we expect one of three possibilities: 1) the world's population will continue to be more or less located where their ancestors were in 2,000 AD; 2) there would be a homogenization of different peoples in currently affluent nations such as the United States but the rest of the world having the same peoples as now; 3) if the world achieves a common standard of living in 3000 AD (an unlikely prospect) then the peoples of the world will generally remain in their current regions. An additional factor that appears likely to occur is a movement of peoples caused by rising sea levels due to global warming. First low-lying areas such as Bangladesh may become unlivable. Secondly, Siberia and northern Canada and Europe will become open to large scale colonization. As Alaska shows, these areas have a great agricultural potential due to the lengthy summer days. These areas also have major natural resources – energy and minerals – that will benefit the world's population.

4. We are now aware that changes are taking place in the genetics of Man. Some of this is natural; some of this is the result of environmental degradation. In 3000 AD it is reasonable to expect that the genetics of Man will be largely the same as now. But we also expect a greater incidence of birth defects passed through the generations unless the environment is cleaned. If the environment does not improve we would also expect greater needs for medical efforts to alleviate the resulting ills. Will Man have greater intellectual abilities? We believe that Man, on the average, will be little changed. We note that Man has not progressed significantly intellectually in the past 1,000 years. There are more highly educated people but genius in the Arts and Sciences has not increased.[23] Thus technical and scientific knowledge will be greater but the intelligence of their practitioners will be the same on average. Based on

---

[23] Those who point to Ptolomaic Astronomy as primitive should consider the fact that it is based on complex geometrical mathematics and its derided epicycles are really a geometric form of Fourier analysis. Fourier analysis was developed in the 19th century and it is intellectually less difficult then the complex geometry of epicycles. One can phenomenologically approximate the curved paths of planets in the sky by using curves within curves (epicycles) geometrically, or by Fourier analysis.

the trends of the past 1,000 years it does not seem reasonable to believe that morality/ethics will be at a higher level than at present. Indeed the drift of Man in these areas would appear to be downward.

5. The progress of Man technically is rising. We expect that Man will probably have colonies on the moon, Mars, large planetoids in the asteroid belt, and research stations on the moons of Jupiter and Saturn. This progress will happen through the use of nuclear rockets or fusion rockets. Computer technology will have reached a high level and there is a strong possibility that intelligent robots will be developed. If so, then a moral issue will arise, as well as an economic issue. Should they be treated as equivalents to Man and accorded the rights of people? Will they displace people from jobs and effectively compete with Man? Today automated factories exist that have eliminated large numbers of jobs.

6. The size of the world population in 3000 AD will have a major impact on all aspects of world civilization(s). It would appear the population range would extend from the 9 billion predicted for 2050 down to perhaps 1 billion if a major population decline should occur. Having seen several potential epidemics arising in Asia in recent years, and being at the time of what may be a major epidemic – Ebola – currently largely in Africa with a mortality rate that could be as high as 70% or more, the possibility of a major population decline due to disease is present. This was discussed in section 3.1. The major point of that discussion, which bears repeating, is the increasing risk of major epidemics due to the increasing population. Firstly, a larger population provides a larger "growing area" for viruses and their mutations. Secondly, a larger population, of necessity, is more crowded facilitating the spread of virulent disease. Thirdly, the continuing growth of travel, particularly via air, makes the spread of disease more rapid. Fourthly, the growth in animal herds – especially pigs and chickens – makes the probability of deadly virus variants much larger. Fifthly, global warming will increase the area of tropical disease-carrying mosquitos to more northern areas increasing the area of life-long debilitating diseases such as West Nile disease, eastern equine encephalitis, and so on.

The impact of population changes – either increases or decreases will be profound affecting all aspects of civilized life.

7. Thus 3000 AD is not likely to see an end to war, poverty, pain, suffering, racism, tyranny, evil, crime, political conflicts, societal instability, injustice, and intolerance; and see a prosperous happy, harmonious world. Rather it would seem that it will be more advanced technically but with a continuation of old troubles and possibly a host of new ones. Humanity will not be much changed, so, in all probability, the condition of humanity will not change much either except in superficial technical ways. If disasters of the sort of chapter 3 happen within the next thousand years then the state of Man will be worse than at present.

4.2 Economic Conditions in 3000 AD

It is difficult to estimate economic conditions in 3000 AD because of important factors that could occur in the next thousand years: disasters mentioned in chapter 3 and above, as well as possible unknown factors. We can examine the current situation and attempt an extrapolation based on likely events and a lack of serious disasters.

4.2.1 Present World Economic Situation

The growth of prosperity in Asia and Europe is a welcome event but it has become clear that much of it was at the expense of the United States and other wealthy countries. Most people hope that all the countries in the world will eventually reach a common high standard of living not unlike that which the United States has enjoyed in recent decades on average. Such a world would have much less reason for warfare and a world at peace would be a likely prospect.

However this dream cannot be accomplished for several reasons. Given the world's population of six billion and the fact that the United States consumes 40% of the world's production while having only about 5% of the world's population, world production would have to increase by a factor of roughly 8 for the average world standard of living to be that of the US. Eight times more food, *eight times more housing, eight times more industry, and so on. Clearly, an impossible task for the earth to achieve and sustain.*

Thus the year 3000 AD world economic situation will range between two extremes barring major technical advances: 1) if the world population declines to about one billion it would be possible for a general prosperity approaching the current standard of living of the United States. A disastrous decline could be the result of a series of major catastrophes that would make prosperity a pyrrhic victory. We are already seeing slow population declines in countries such as Japan with their attendant economic and social ills; 2) the world's population could range upwards from the current level – the result would be a world filled with the economic inequities that we currently see and, most likely, wars and conflicts for economic benefits.

4.2.2 Environmental Conditions

We must accept the fact that the world today is at its environmental limits. The degradation of the environment at today's production levels is obvious: water and land are increasing polluted (poisoned). In particular, the oceans are being polluted with heavy metals, plastics, sludge, oil and so on. We are entering a period of man-made global warming, increasing air pollution, increasing birth defects and educational disabilities, and other signs of an overstressed and precipitously declining environment. As the population grows to nine billion in 2050 we can expect to see conditions worsen.

And the terrible fact is that we cannot change these trends without massive efforts that will cause a major lowering of the standard of living for all nations. *These facts "everybody" feels but political leaders in every country cannot voice them without causing major population unrest.* Can the leaders of China or India say they can never reach the American standard of living without causing their peoples to lose hope and perhaps turn to unscrupulous demagogues who will promise anything to achieve power? Can an American president say that universal lifetime health care, while maintaining current high standards of medical quality, is not economically feasible over the long term?

Clearly world leaders avoid stating the realities of the world situation and put in place "programs of hope" that promise eventual benefits but in reality cannot lead to the nirvanas they boldly promise.

The most significant and most understated problem facing the earth is the need to balance production with effective waste disposal. Manufacturing in all its facets is producing products, which often require waste disposal methods whose costs are comparable to the costs of their production. The cost of waste disposal must be built in to the price of products.

Given these environmental facts the world of 3000 AD can only achieve a successful prosperity if the world population significantly declines from its present levels. The possibilities and consequences of this decline are discussed above.

An important point is the process of depopulation. If it happens naturally through a disaster then we must make do with it. If it must be politically mandated as in China today then how will we decide the reduction country by country, people by people. This would require a strong world government to implement it. And the possibility of wars and internal conflicts would be great. Given the world social climate today and most likely for the next few hundred years it appears that any downsizing will only take place through natural disasters. Barring disasters the most likely scenario for 3000 AD is an overcrowded planet with massive waste problems and large numbers of impoverished (half-starved) people.

4.2.3 Zero Sum World Economy Today. The Future?

Until recently growth and development were the engines of prosperity. Now we must realize a change is necessary to a zero sum economy where *"every dollar spent on production must be matched by a dollar spent on recycling and environmental protection."*

Further, the Chinese program of population limitation should be taken up by the other nations of the world in an appropriate form. The western nations of Europe and North America have stable or declining populations if the immigrant populations are not counted. The countries in Asia, South America, Central America, and Africa need to strongly encourage population limitation with the spirit of the Chinese model but not necessarily with the methods of the Chinese government.

An eventual downsizing of the earth's population to about one+ billion by 3000 AD appears to be required if we wish a high standard of living for all, combined with a clean, stable world environment over the long term.

4.2.4 The Effect of a Declining Population in the Next Thousand Years

Downsizing the population of a nation or a planet is an undertaking fraught with dangers. Japan is experiencing some of those difficulties as its population declines, and ages. Economic problems include the cost of supporting an aging population. The major burden falls on the working, youthful part of the population whose percentage of the total population is decreasing.

There is a more subtle cultural issue associated with aging. The creativity and cultural progress generated by the more youthful part of the population is less strong as the relative proportion of younger people declines.

In the case of our world, the population will grow from the current six billion to nine billion in 2050 (a figure which cannot be changed except by drastic events). Then the population must decrease to about one billion over the next one thousand years to achieve a maintainable, high standard of living for all. One can only expect that near totalitarian means will have to be used to achieve this goal. The result of this plan will be to profoundly affect the world's economy and the world's ability to engage in major projects such as space exploration and scientific research.

At present large scale scientific and space projects are carried on by nations with large populations with the economic wherewithal to pay for these projects. Large-scale projects cost little for large countries on a per capita basis. A small population necessarily will have a "small" overall economy and will not be able to finance major projects such as space exploration at a low per capita cost in the manner that we see currently unfolding in the US, EU, Chinese, and Indian space programs.

Lastly, if the earth's population is reduced to about one billion in 3000 AD it is possible that "overshoot" may occur and the population might further decline to unacceptable levels. An excellent example of this possibility is the latter phases of the Roman Empire when many areas including Italy experienced large declines in population. Augustus Caesar noting the decline in birth rates amongst the Roman population started the practice of paying bonuses to parents for having children. More recently, France, Germany, and other modern European countries have experienced continuing population declines.

Thus the world of 3000 AD will have a delicate balance to maintain a population of one billion should a population downsizing occur.

4.2.5 Waste Management in 3000 AD

If the world population is large then the most likely possibility is seriously polluted land and oceans, a polluted food supply, massive numbers of birth defects and health problems, and a fierce competition for natural resources and agricultural land. If the world undertakes a massive effort to recycle waste, and dispose of waste in land areas unsuitable for human purposes (such as regions in the Rocky mountains, deep unused mines, and large deserts then there is hope for a cleaner environment.

4.2.6 Increased Maintenance and Rebuilding Costs

If the world population remains the same or grows there will be increased maintenance requirements for roads and buildings. A classic example is the US federal highway system which will require increasing maintenance efforts – particularly bridge maintenance, which have already started collapsing in various areas. Dams, major water pipes, power plants and skyscrapers also will require major maintenance or rebuilding. These costs will sap the economy significantly.

If the population increases, then more building/construction will be needed and current areas with substandard buildings will have to be rebuilt.

If the population decreases substantially, then large areas of existing structures will have to be destroyed or allowed to revert to nature – perhaps increasing the amount of arable land.

4.3 Technology in 3000 AD

The ever accelerating rate of technological advances gives us the hope that the technology developed over the next thousand years may increase the general prosperity of the world and resolve the many problems facing us now and the new problems that undoubtedly will face us in the future. We see that the world needs to miniaturize many items of everyday life to save on resources and lower costs, to move to packaging that will be degradable thus minimizing the massive pollution of the land and oceans, and to develop methods to clean the accumulated waste (particularly toxic waste) that has been so harmful to humanity (birth defects and health problems). Technology can be the key to a better future where we can better cultivate and exploit the world's resources and work to improve the intellectual and cultural capacity of Man so that 3000 AD will be part of an era of a new renaissance for Man.

4.3.1 New Advances Based on New More Powerful Computers

As computers become more powerful and cost effective it is becoming possible to use them in new ways: accident prevention in automobiles, medical procedures, improved hearing and vision technology, sophisticated alarm systems for homes and businesses, factory automation particularly in labor intensive tasks, improved agricultural cultivation and harvesting (no more stoop labor), making water usage more efficient in home and industry, and in many more applications.

4.3.2 Miniaturization of Devices and Artifacts

Many items that are somewhat bulky and may require powerful battery power can be miniaturized lowering their cost of manufacture and utilization of natural resources such as copper and gold. Miniaturized devices lower waste disposal costs.

However because of the size of Man certain items are not miniaturizable: houses, cars, ships, roads, and so on. The creation, use and disposal of such items can be improved by the development of new materials that will lower their costs of production and disposal when no longer needed. So one can hope that new materials technology will improve this area of need in the future.

4.3.3 Degradable Packaging

Degradable packaging is a major need. It contributes mightily to waste. Much of it takes a very long to revert to a natural state. Materials technology can develop new forms of packaging that do not contribute to waste disposal problems and environmental degradation.

4.3.4 Improved Cleanup Methods for Accumulated (Toxic) Waste

There has been some progress in developing bacteria that consume waste. This is a bioengineering and materials science problem that can eventually help bring the earth to a healthier state.

4.3.5 A Possible Decline of Science and Technology

In our discussions we have assumed that technological advance will continue in the future. While this has been true in the past two hundred years there are occasions in history where science and technology have been brought to a halt. The best example is the Roman conquest of Alexandria, Egypt in which the Library of Alexandria was destroyed and its group of scientists killed or dispersed. These scientists were working on steam engines, astronomy, mathematics and other areas of science. Their work was destroyed. Scientific advance halted. The murder of Archimedes in Syracuse, Sicily, perhaps the greatest scientist of his day, also decisively ended a major area of scientific effort. Together science in the West was brought to a halt for over a millennium.

Can such a disaster happen in the future? Yes, if there is a global atomic war or if a catastrophic event of world-wide significance occurred such as a collision with a massive asteroid or a combination of major volcanic eruptions. Thus the future has seeds of uncertainty for the future progress of science. The probabilities of these events are low but not zero.

4.4 Civilizational/Political Conditions in 3000 AD

The world of 3000 AD can be a paradise of sorts or a cesspool of struggling humanity. Its state depends partly on Man's efforts and Nature's activity. If we compare 1000 AD with the present we see the vast changes that have taken place. But when we read Chaucer's Canterbury Tales or Boccaccio's works we see that human nature is largely the same as at present. We also see the struggle for survival is largely the same – although slightly improved by government and law. We also see that security is still a major issue for many peoples in the midst of belligerence and lawlessness. We also see that corruption in business and government still exists.

National and civilizational conflicts still beleaguer us. The expansion of Islam and its wars with other nations are still present. The expansionism of Russia is still present. The actions of China to expand its domains can be seen.

And yet there is hope that the nations and civilizations of the earth will come to realize that life is more precious than these conflicts and aggressions; hope that Man will see that creation is more important than any benefits that might accrue from destruction; hope that peace and tranquility will lead Man to further his intellectual and social goals – that we may at last see a lasting peace embodied by a renaissance in the spirit of Man.

4.4.1 A Continuation of Existing Civilizations?

With the preceding sentiments in mind we ask whether the current civilizations of the world will exist in 3000 AD. If they do exist will their existence be to Man's benefit? Or will they precipitate conflicts with the more powerful, more cruel weaponry that technology will undoubtedly devise in the next thousand years?

It appears that there may well be a loosely united world government – the United Nations or a successor government – that will have some powers related to the preservation of peace and the regulation of world trade and finance. One might consider it to be analogous to the early days of the United States where state governments had sizeable powers to manage their own internal affairs. Without projecting further it seems that this government will proceed to gain in strength leading perhaps to a major conflict not unlike a civil war of the sort experienced by the United States.

The civilizations that exist now seem likely to exist in 3000 AD. Chinese civilization has persisted for about 5000 years. It is unlikely to become "homogenized" with other civilizations except for some cultural and scientific cross fertilization with other civilizations. India also has a strong civilizational identity that seems unlikely to disappear into a world civilization. It also will borrow from other civilizations but will retain its overall uniqueness based on 4000 years of history. Islam has captured the hearts of its adherents to the extent that it is also very likely to retain its identity as a civilization. Russian civilization has a unity of spirit and a remembrance of a long, tragic history. The strength of Russia and the unity of the people of Russian civilization make it likely that it will retain its identity. Western civilization has been declining for the past hundred years. This decline is apparent in social trends and in its declining population. The emigration of large numbers of people of other civilizations will cause Western civilization to change significantly although it will continue to exist as long as its technical prowess continues to excel.

Africa today is divided and filled with problems and conflicts. However there is an unstated unification taking place that will eventually lead to a sub-Saharan African civilization. This author has noticed massive interchanges between nations taking place throughout sub-Saharan Africa from South Africa and Mozambique to Ghana and the other nations of West and Central Africa. Eventually an African cultural unification will occur and perhaps a united sub-Saharan African nation will develop.

Thus we expect that the major civilizations of the world will still exist in 3000 AD although they will have substantial cultural and technological interchanges and a type of unity forge by the Internet and its potential successors. A true World civilization does not seem likely by 3000 AD although in the distant future a World civilization will be forged.

The author views the appearance of a true World civilization with some concern because the diversity of civilizations enriches the world. A unified World civilization may become a static civilization without the creative growth that has marked past civilizations in history. The one great advantage of a World civilization is a lasting peace. Perhaps that overrides the danger of a homogenized static civilization.

4.4.2 An End to Man's Expansion?

In 3000 AD the Siberian and Arctic regions will be suitable for colonization and resource exploitation. However these regions, although large, will eventually be "civilized" giving us a world without room for further expansion. Arnold Toynbee, in his monumental treatise on civilization Toynbee (1961), pointed out that "new land" has always been the ground for new civilizations and the growth of existing civilizations. Thus a "filled" earth portends a possible end to growth in Man's civilizations. The obvious solution to this possible problem is to expand into space and develop Space civilizations.[24] The possibilities in space are enormous and will yield an unlimited future for humanity.

4.5 Exhaustion of Natural Resources?

At present there are localized shortages of food, water, and other natural resources. These shortages are primarily based on poverty in underdeveloped countries. In 3000 AD if the world population is not substantially lower it is probable that the areas with major shortages will be much larger. Today there is competition for natural resources: the mineral and oil wealth of Africa (China

---
[24] See Blaha (2009a), (2009b), 2010), (2013a), (2014b), (2014c).

and the West), Siberia (China and Russia), the East China Sea's oil potential (China and neighboring countries), Central Asia's oil (China, Russia and the West), the Arctic's oil and minerals (bordering countries), and so on. Competition for water also exists: Nile River water (Egypt, Sudan, and Ethiopia), water for California and the American Southwest, clean water for China, and so on. Food is in short supply in many parts of the world and increasingly expensive. Competition for food for a large world population may become very intense. Twenty-five per cent of the world's arable land is seriously degraded. By 3000 AD one can expect a significantly larger portion of the world's land will be degraded to meet the needs of a larger world population and as a result of industrial development.

With all these factors in mind it is clear that world resources will be seriously reduced in 3000 AD compared to the present with a population level equal to, or greater than, the present world population. The result can only be a fierce scramble for world resources whether or not the world is politically unified. And the standard of living inequalities will continue to exist. The more affluent areas and countries will resist lowering their standard of living for the benefit of the poorer segment of the world's population. The result will probably be a continuation of conflicts for resources. A true unification of the world based on an adequate standard of living for all people, and a stable world economy, appear to be unlikely.

4.6 The Increasing Probability of a Pandemic

As this book is being written the Ebola epidemic is largely confined to West Africa. Perhaps it will be brought to an end by quarantine or by the development of an Ebola vaccine. The growing range of Ebola outbreaks over the past decade is a worrisome trend. If Ebola should become a pandemic then one can expect the world's population to be cut in half and world society to suffer a crushing blow: to life, to all the features of modern life, to the psychology of the various peoples and to the future progress of Man.

Even if Ebola is conquered, we clearly can foresee (point 6 of section 4.1) that we are in for more major disease and pandemic. Thus the year 3000 AD may be an occasion of sadness of the sort seen in the Black Death that decimated Europe in centuries past. We hope that the world will grow and prosper but we must be aware of the continuing challenge of the future. Nothing is certain. Not now. Not then.

New Support for the Superorganism Macro-Theory of Civilizations from New Peruvian, Pre-Mayan, Mayan, Anatolian, and Early Egyptian Data

5. New Archaeological Data Supporting Our Macro-Theory

Since the appearance[25] of our comprehensive theory of civilizations based on the thermodynamics of the resources that fuel civilizations and confirmed by the history of over fifty civilizations located in Africa, Asia, the Americas and Europe, new archaeological and climate data has appeared for Peruvian, Pre-Mayan, Mayan, Anatolian, and Early Egyptian civilizations that strongly supports both our theory, and its foundation in the thermodynamic energetics of civilizations.

The proof of any theory is its solid grounding in fundamental principles and its consistency with the known data. The proof is further supported when new data appears that agrees with the predictions of the theory.

In the following chapters we will consider new data and show that it agrees with our theory. This additional confirmation, and its prior success in accounting for the history of over fifty civilizations, leads us to conclude we have the correct, precise theory of civilizations – knowing that chance events will occur that appear to differ from the theory. (Chance events also happen in Physics experiments that differ from established Physics theories. They are usually discarded.)

It is of particular interest that our theory of civilizations is based on the same principles that govern the behavior of superorganisms such as social insects: ants, bees, and so on. Thus Man partakes of the same principles of Nature that describe other species – insects, bacteria, some plant species as well as mammalian and fish species.

---

[25] *Supercivilizations*, Blaha (2010).

6. New Data for Pre-Classical and Classical Mayan Civilizations

In this chapter we will show that new weather data for Classical Mayan theory supports the basis and predictions of our theory. We will also show that new data on Pre-Classical Mayan times supports our theory of a link between Pre-Classical Mayan civilization and Peruvian (Andean) civilizations.

6.1 Weather Data for Classical Mayan Civilization Supporting the Energetic Basis of the Theory and its Predictions for Classical Mayan Civilization

In 2002 (and subsequent books) we described the application of our theory to Classical Mayan civilization. The discussion[26] in Blaha (2002b) is:

> A sequence of Mayan civilizations existed in Central America. We will begin by examining Classical Mayan civilization (223 BC – 900 AD). It is fairly well known and will be seen to conform to our theory.
>
> #### 6.2.1 Central America: Classical Mayan: 223 BC – 900 AD
> Classical Mayan civilization was thought to have grown in isolation in Central America. It appeared to have begun with a roughly 134 year Startup period of major growth beginning around 223 BC. Great cities were built such as El Mirador. Teotihuacan was also founded in the first century BC. Mayan civilization then went through three and a half cycles of routs and rallies similar to our civilization theory.
>
> The last cycle was dominated by constant wars between Tikal and Calakmul that culminated in the decline of Mayan civilization. Tikal's conquest of Calakmul around 700 AD started the last stage of decline that ended in the complete abandonment of the Mayan cities around 900 AD. It has been suggested that an extraordinary dry spell from 800 AD to 1000 AD was a major factor in the collapse as well.[27] Warfare is often stimulated by competition for food and a long dry spell leads to a scarcity of food and thus famine.

---

[26] Bracketed items [] are explanatory insertions in this book and are not in Blaha (2002b).
[27] D. Hodell et al, Science **292**, 1367 (2001).

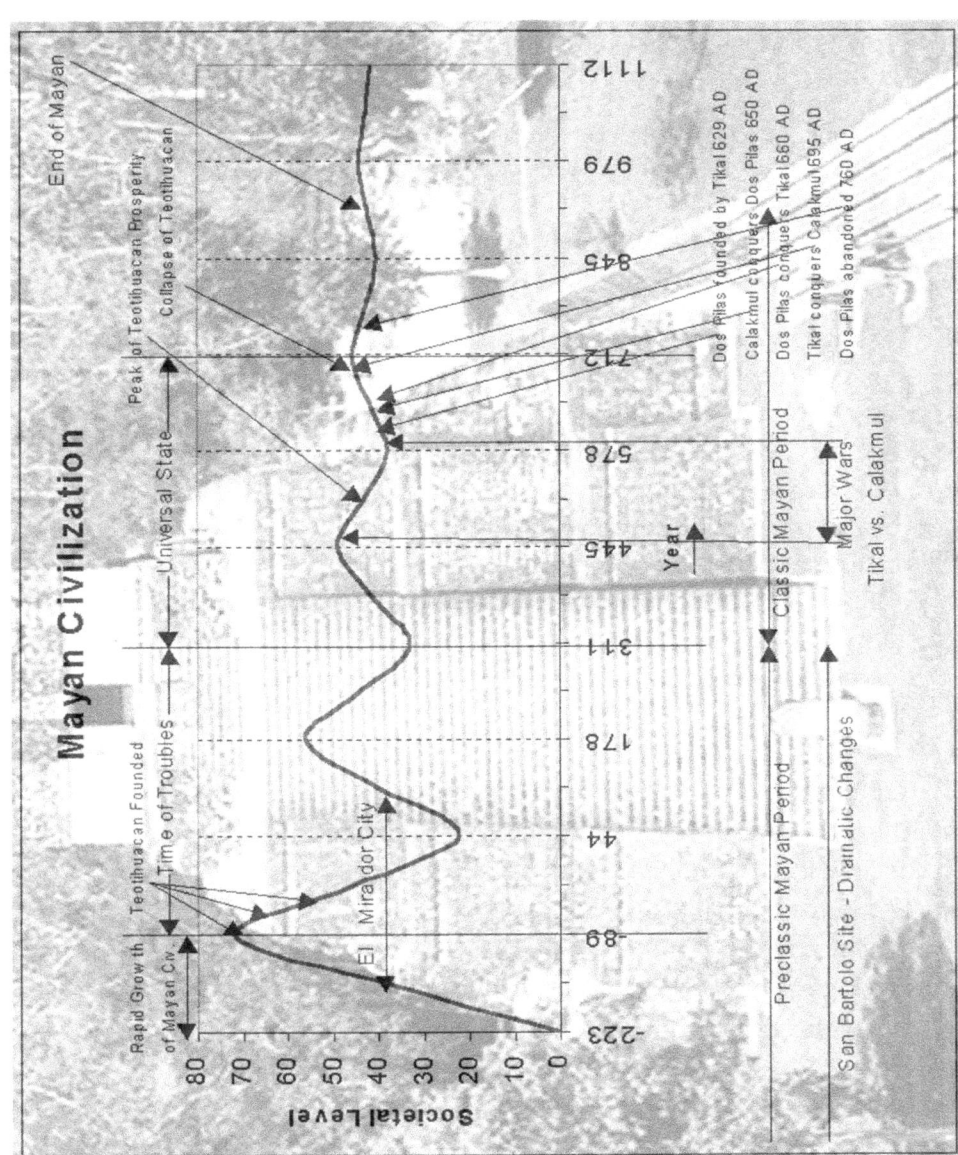

Figure 6.6. Classical Mayan civilization growth/Societal Level compared to historical events. [The oscillating line is called the Societal level or Growth rate.][28]

---

[28] From Blaha (2002b).

These historical findings appear to support civilization theory. Previously Mayan history was viewed as a collection of random wars between city-states that ended around 900 AD in a mass exodus from the cities. It now appears that Mayan civilization underwent a civilizational pattern of development.

The growth/Societal Level curve for Mayan civilization can be determined by one parameter – the point where the civilization began its Startup. In Blaha (2002B) we set the beginning of Mayan civilization to 223 BC.[29] ... Fig. 6.6 compares $S_{Mayan}(t)$ [called the Growth curve rate in the energetics approach Blaha (2010)] with known historical events. It shows good agreement with historical events.

Recently, new detailed rainfall data has appeared[30] that correlates well with our curve displayed in Fig. 6.6 above. Fig. 6.1 below shows the data of Kennett et al and Fig. 6.2 shows a superposition of Fig. 6.6 above from Blaha (2002b) and Fig. 6.1. There is a clear correlation between the rainfall data and our growth rate curve. Remembering that our energetics model relates the growth rate to the availability and utilization of resources, and remembering that rainfall is the essential ingredient for crop success or failure, we see that the Mayan civilization's ups and down's followed rainfall abundance – but with lag times as abundance builds up or shortfalls lead to poor times.

Correlated periods of ups and downs of rainfall and Classical Mayan are:

- From 20 BC to 80 AD there was a period of larger amounts of rainfall that led to a turn around and a rise in growth rate from 44 AD to 178 AD.
- The subsequent lower average rainfall from 110 AD to 320 AD led to a decline in growth from 178 AD to 311 AD.
- The subsequent larger average rainfall from 320 AD to 420 AD led to a rise in growth from 311 AD to 445 AD.
- The big rainfall drop around 420 AD led to a mild decline.
- The subsequent abrupt sharp highs and lows of rainfall allowed the Mayans to progress through mild rises and falls until a major fall in rainfall effectively led to the end of Mayan civilization.

---

[29] There is strong evidence for a prior pre-classical Mayan civilization based on the research of a team led by Professor F. Estrada-Belli (Vanderbilt University).
[30] Douglas J. Kennett et al, Science **338**, 788 (2012).

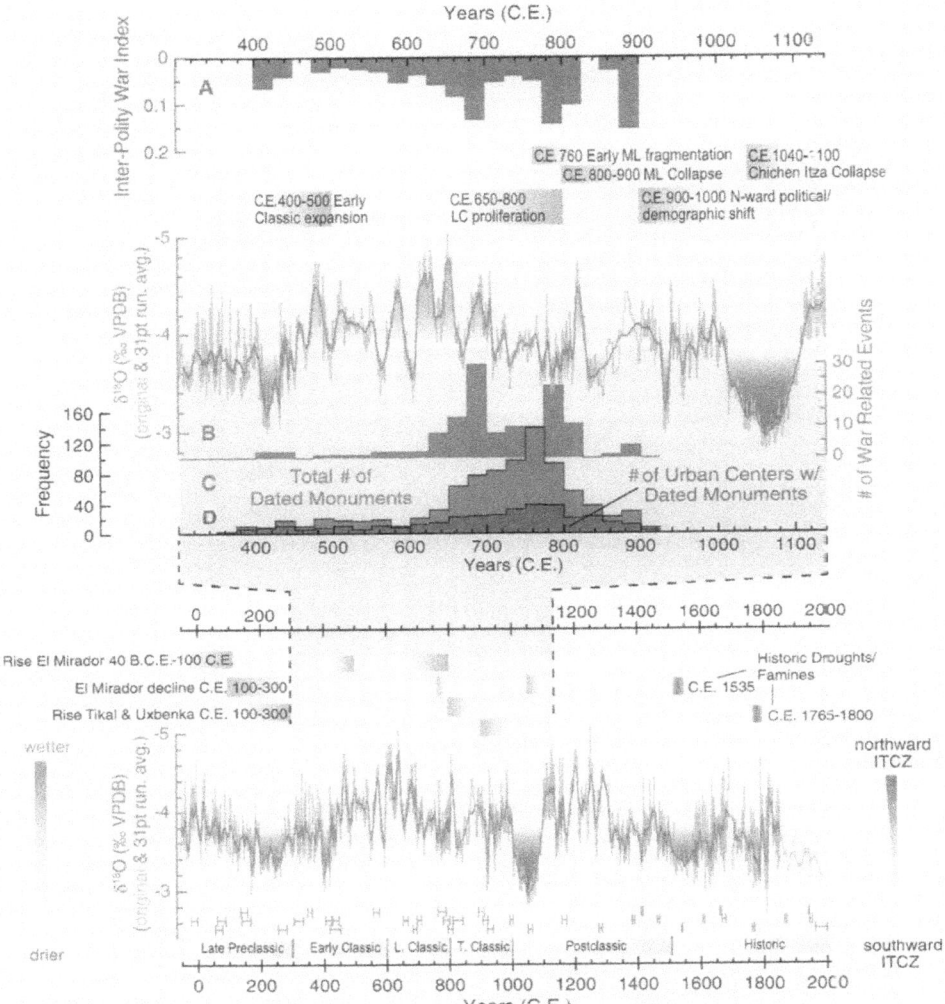

Fig. 2. (Bottom) YOK-I $\delta^{18}O$ climate record spanning the past 2000 years (40 B.C.E. to 2006 C.E.) shown relative to Maya chronology and major historical events. Blue bars just below the $\delta^{18}O$ curve indicate the small error for each of the 40 U-Th dates used to constrain the chronology of the $\delta^{18}O$ climate record (10). Drier-than-average conditions during this interval are shown in orange. Two historically recorded droughts in the 16th- and 18th-century C.E. accord well with the YOK-I record, and the earliest multidecadal drought in the record (200 to 300 C.E.) corresponds with decline of the large center of El Mirador and a major sociopolitical reorganization in the ML. (Top) The YOK-I $\delta^{18}O$ climate record between 300 and 1140 C.E. shown relative to major historic events along with (A) An interpolity warfare index based on the number of war-related events between Maya sites or rulers relative to the total number of events recorded during each interval. (B) Raw number of war-related events. (C) Frequency distribution of long-count dated monuments in the ML. (D) Total number of urban centers with dated monuments through time as a proxy for the development and disintegration of complex polities in the ML. All hieroglyphic data are from the Maya Hieroglyphic database (raw data is available in the supplementary materials) (28) and are binned in 25-year intervals. The light gray line denotes uncertainties in the 20th-century $\delta^{18}O$ record (10).

Figure 6.1. A measure of rainfall patterns in Mayan times from Douglas J. Kennett et al, Science 338, 788 (2012).

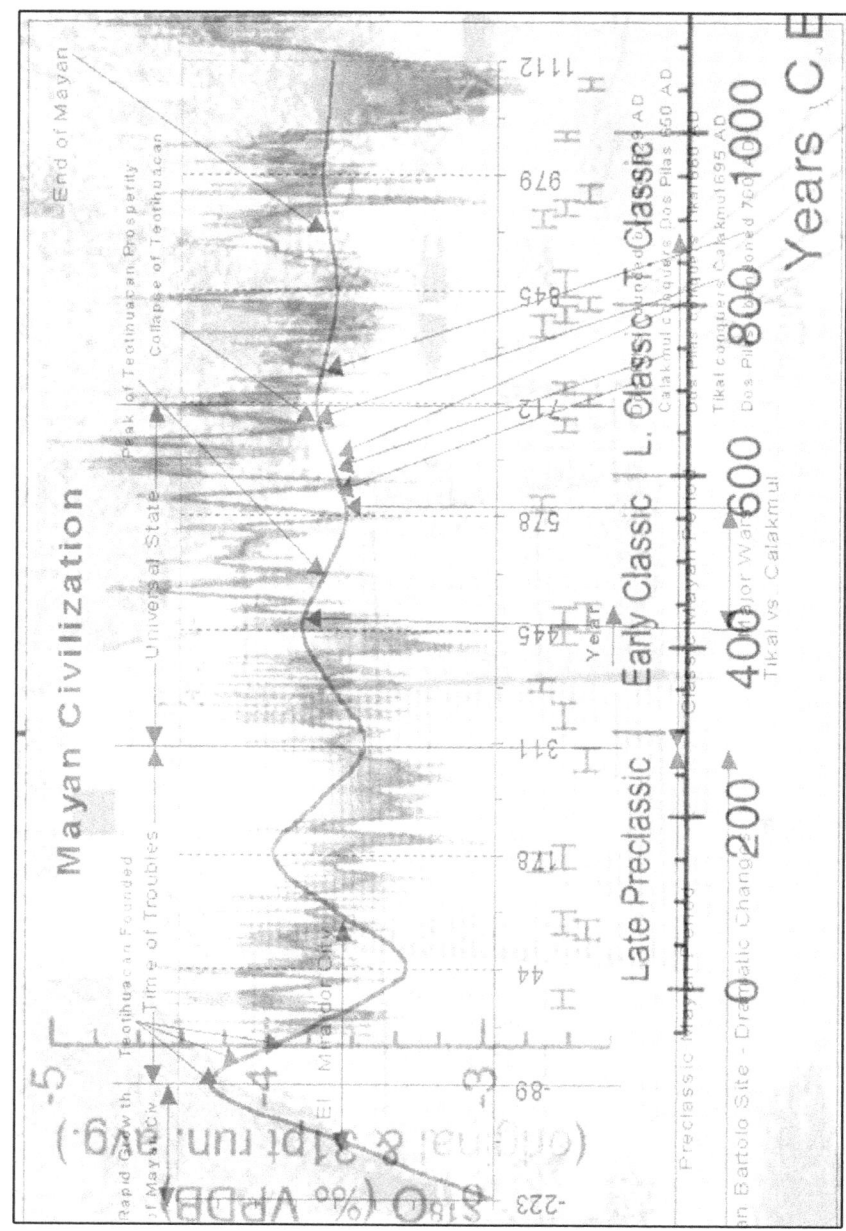

Figure 6.2. A superposition of Figs. 6.1 and 6.6 above showing a correlation between rainfall and the growth rate of Classical Mayan civilization.

Hodell et al[31] has suggested that an extraordinary drought from 800 AD to 1000 AD was a major factor in its collapse. Warfare is often stimulated by a competition for food. A long drought leads to a scarcity of food, thus famine and an abandonment of cities that no longer have sources of food.

Hodell et al also found major but less severe droughts in the periods: 475 BC – 250 BC and 125 AD - 210 AD.

Thus we see that resources – in this case rainfall – affect the ups and downs of civilizations – particularly in the case of a semi-isolated civilization like Classical Mayan civilization.

6.2 New Support for a Link between Peruvian Civilizations and Pre-Classical Mayan Civilization

In Blaha (2010) and earlier books we developed a connection between various Peruvian (Andean) civilizations, and Pre-Classical Mayan civilization. We present part of that discussion below (with some irrelevant omissions and some explanatory notes added in brackets):

6.2.2 Central America: Pre-Classical Mayan: 1168 BC – 250 BC

A number of pyramids and building complexes of the little-known Pre-Classical Mayan civilization were constructed before the 475 BC – 250 BC drought. It appears that Pre-Classical Mayan civilization ended somewhere within the 475 BC – 250 BC drought. Since the drought was less severe than the drought that ended Classical Mayan civilization, it was possible for a new Mayan civilization Startup, Classical Mayan civilization, to begin (after a brief interregnum) in 223 BC.

At present, knowledge of the Pre-Classical Mayan period is beginning to become available. We know of the sophistication of its artwork. But we know little else. So we will use the date, at which one of its major cities, Cival, was started to set the date of the *first peak after the beginning of the Universal State period*. This will enable us to estimate a Startup date.[See Fig. 1.1 for an explanation of these terms – due to Toynbee.] The time of this peak = 134 years (Startup period) + 400 years (Time of Troubles) + 134 years (rally period to first peak) = 638 years.

Cival started about 500 BC. Therefore the Startup date we will use is 500 + 638 = 1168 BC. [See Blaha (2010) or earlier books for more information on this calculation.] Is this Startup date reasonable? The year 0 in the Maya calendar is 3114 BC – almost 2000 years prior to the estimated Startup date. More importantly, it is known that Mayans lived in villages in 1500 BC.

---

[31] D. Hodell et al, Science **292**, 1367 (2001).

Thus a [civilization] Startup of 1168 BC seems reasonable since it could not have been much earlier than the 12th century BC.

If Pre-Classical Mayan civilization followed the civilization pattern then the civilization would have ended 934 years later in 234 BC just after the end of a drought.

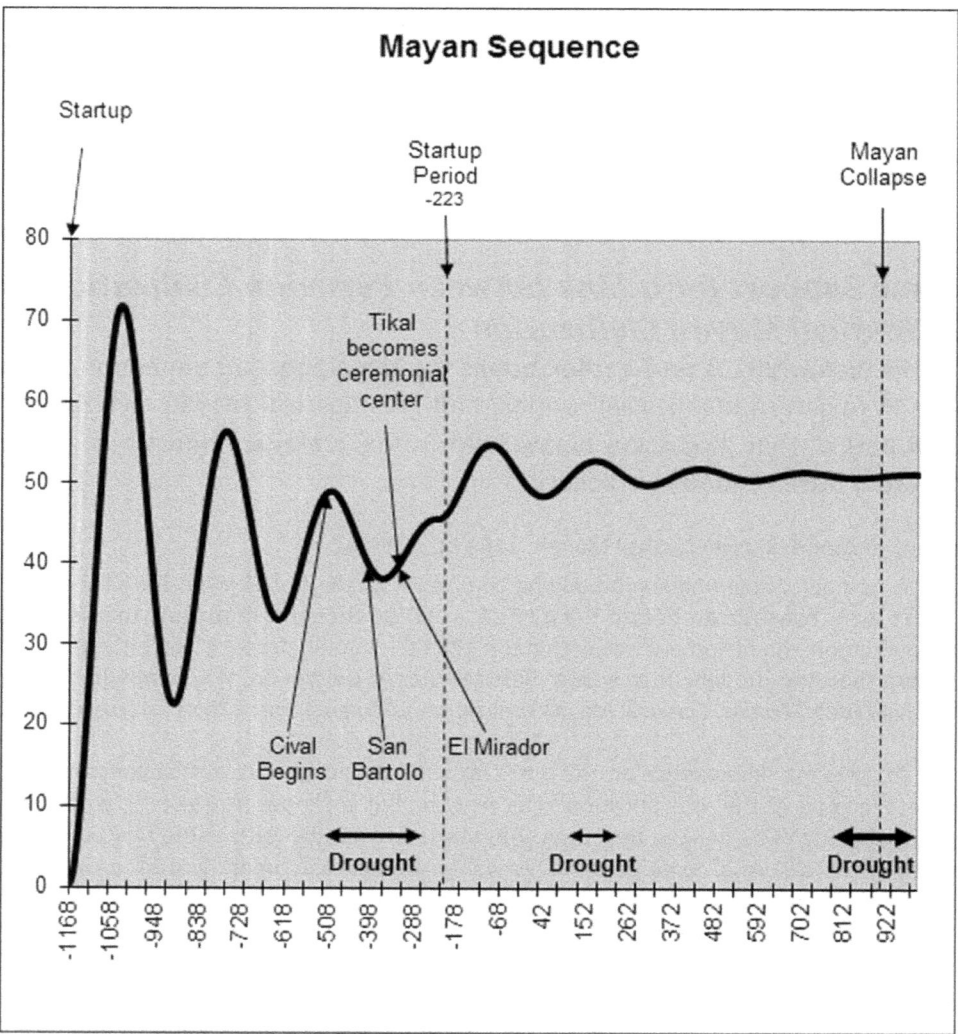

Figure 6.7. The growth/Societal Level of the Mayan sequence of civilizations with some Preclassic events shown. See Fig. 6.6 for the growth of Classical Mayan civilization and its events.

The following facts are known about Pre-Classical Mayan civilization:

- South American influenced pottery has been found in Panama with dates as early as 2130 BC.
- Pre-Classical Mayan civilization occupied Guatemala, Belize, and southern Mexico.
- Advanced Mayan artifacts have been found in the Guatemalan Highlands, and El Salvador dating to 500 BC.
- Cival, a city in Guatemala, was started in 500 BC. (Artifacts have been dated to 500 BC.) Its prime was reached in 150 BC at which time it had about 10,000 inhabitants. It had pyramids and a large building complex.
- San Bartolo, in the Petén lowlands, Guatemala, has large, sophisticated artifacts dating back to 400 BC, and Mayan handwriting[32] samples dating back to 200 BC.
- El Mirador in northern Petén, Guatemala was founded in 300 BC and had a population estimated at 100,000 at its peak in 150 BC – 150 AD. Its massive construction dwarfs Tikal.
- Tikal, in the Petén region, was a village from 900 BC to 300 BC. It then became a ceremonial center. Tikal underwent a period of major rebuilding and prosperity starting in 200 BC. The immense Lost World Pyramid was built in the period from 900 BC to 300 BC.

[See Fig. 6.7 above for the growth in the Pre-Classical and Classical Mayan civilizations.]

An Andean-Mayan Connection
Although we commonly think of Mayan and Andean civilizations as distinct and separate (and this is true to a large extent), there is clear archaeological evidence that trade connections existed between coastal Andean cultures and Central American, and Mexican cultures, as far back as 2500 BC to 3000 BC, and probably earlier.

While Andean cultures are separated from Guatemala and Mexico by mountains, deserts, and "impenetrable" jungles, coastal travel in boats is comparatively easy. Indeed we have evidence of Colombian and Mexican influence in Ecuador, an outlying region of Andean civilizations. There is also evidence of Andean civilizations' influence in archaeological finds in the area of Parita Bay, Panama dating back to 2130 BC.

The exchanges between Andean civilizations and Central America raise the question: did the trade with Andean civilizations provide the "spark" that ignited Pre-Classical Mayan civilization from a region of villages in 1500 BC. The situation might be similar to the beginning of the European Renaissance due to the transfer of ideas and art from Classical Greece and Rome.

The time frames of trade and civilization appear to be in agreement:

- Trade between Central America and Andean civilizations starting at least c. 2500 BC.

---

[32] W. Saturno, D. Stuart, B. Beltran, Science Express (Online) 1/5/2006; and references therein.

- Evidence of trade exchanges up the coast to the Bay of Panama by 2130 BC.

- Evidence of trade exchanges up to Chiapas, Mexico by 1500 BC.

- Caral civilization lasts from 2700 BC to 1800 BC and the successor to the north Casma civilization lasts from 1500 BC to 400 BC. Both civilizations consumed seafood in large quantities and had extensive trading operations. Their sea-going capabilities are thus not in doubt.

- The city of Ocós (1500–1200 BC) had highly developed pottery and the first temple pyramid in Central America with a height of 26 feet.[33]

- The Mayans transitioned from villages in 1500 BC to Pre-Classical Mayan civilization c. 1300 BC.

- West Mexican Shaft Tombs (some as far back as 1500BC; most 200 BC – 400 AD are very like Ecuador & Peru. (Meighan & Nicholson, 1989)

- The Coastal Colima (Mexico) Formative Period Capacha Phase (1500 BC) closely resemble s pottery from Ecuador's Machallilla phase[11] (1500 BC – 500 BC) (Kelly, 1980)

- Metallurgy – starts in 1500 BC in Peru highlands; in Columbia in 200 BC (approx.); and introduced into West Mexico around 800 AD. Early West Mexican metallurgy is very similar to South & Central American metallurgy. A clear time line of events.

Thus there is a chain of archaeological evidence supporting a link with the Caral-Casma sequence of civilizations.[described later] Trade was conducted largely in metals, minerals, gems, pottery, cloth and medicinal plants. Therefore one would expect the influence of the Caral and Casma civilizations on Pre-Classical Mayan civilization to be mostly in material goods and production techniques such as methods of pottery making. However the religion and daily life of the Central American peoples could also change based on new ideas brought in by the traders.

It is particularly interesting that the first pyramidal structure in Central America was at Ocós. This structure might have been the prototype for the later pyramids of the Mayans.

One could ask why civilizations didn't develop between the Andean civilizations and Guatemala. The reasons seem to be environmental. Much of the coastline between these regions consists of deserts or jungles with poor soils, a profusion of pests, and hot, humid climates. In

---

[33] Another 30 foot high pyramid appears at the nearby site of Chiapa de Corzo in Chiapas dating to 1700 BC. (Dr. Bruce R. Bachand of Brigham Young University has studied this pyramid and the tombs found within.)

addition much of the Colombian coast consists of small valleys that could not support more than small villages. Thus the origin of the gap between Andean and Central American civilizations.

Figure 6.5. Trade route along the South and Central American coastline from Peru to Mexico with dates of Parita Bay (2130 BC) and Ocós (1500 BC) artifact finds indicated.

Peruvian Fishing Extended to Mexican Coast

In 2013, Inomata et al[34] investigated the origins of lowland Maya civilization in the period from 1000 BC to 700 BC. They found that the origins of

---
[34] Takeshi Inomata et al, Science **340**, 467 (2013).

the Mayan civilizations (Pre-Classical Mayan and Classical Mayan) were from Chiapas, the Pacific coast, and the southern Gulf Coast, and not from the Olmecs as had previously been thought. This discovery confirms the passage quoted above from Blaha (2010) and his earlier books.

We attributed the origins of Pre-Classical Mayan civilization to the significant influence of the fishing fleets of Andean civilizations from Ecuador and Peru. Inomata et al have apparently confirmed the impact of Andean civilizations on Mayan origins. A major point in favor of this concept is the appearance of Andean artifacts at points along the coast up as far as Chiapas, Mexico.

Period		Cal. BC	San Lorenzo/ La Venta	Chiapa de Corzo	Southern Pacific Coast	Ceibal		Political processes and construction events
Preclassic	Late	300	Zapote	Guanacaste	Guillén	Cantutse	2	
		400		Francesa	Frontera		1	
		500	Late Franco				3	La Venta as a major center
		600		Escalera	Escalón	Escoba	2	Spread of E-Group assemblages in the Maya lowlands
	Middle	700	Early Franco	Vista Hermosa	Late Conchas		1	Tikal and Cival E-Group assemblages
		800					3	Spread of MFC patterns in central Chiapas
		900	Late Puente	Dili	Early Conchas	Real	2	Ceibal pyramid and monumental construction La Blanca pyramid?
		1000					1	Ceibal E-Group assemblage
		1100	Early Puente	Cotorra	Jocotal			Ojo de Agua plaza-pyramid complex
	Early	1200						
		1300	San Lorenzo		Cuadros			San Lorenzo as a major center

ig. 2. Chronology of southern Mesoamerica.

Figure 6.3. Major Pre-Classical Mayan sites. From Takeshi Inomata et al, Science 340, 467 (2013).

A more impressive point is the first appearance of a pyramidal structure in Central America at Ocós on the Guatemalan coast not far from Cival. This structure, seemingly suggested by fishermen/trader visitors from Ecuador and Peru, is very likely the prototype for the later pyramids of the Mayans. Thus our theory of Pre-Classical Mayan civilization has strong field support for its origins. [Fig. 6.5 above shows one of the fishing routes to the rich fishing grounds along the Central American coast.]

Fig. 1. Map of southern Mesoamerica with the locations of Ceibal and the sites discussed in the text.

Figure 6.4. Map of Pre-Classical Mayan sites. From Takeshi Inomata et al, Science 340, 467 (2013).

Most impressively, Inomata et al showed that a Pre-Classical Mayan civilization existed by identifying the major structures they built before the Classical Mayan civilization. See Fig. 6.3 for a list of the Pre-Classical sites and Fig. 6.4 for a map of the sites.

This new data shows the existence of Pre-Classical Mayan civilization, and supports our view that major aspects of its origin are due to the influence of fishermen from Andean civilizations.

7. New Data for Peruvian Civilizations

In Blaha (2010) and in our earlier books we discussed the sequence of Peruvian (Andean) civilizations. They have the remarkable feature that they all last for about one thousand years and then expire by just petering out. Even more remarkably the civilizations branch into two consecutive paths: one path of civilization to the north, and the other path to the south. Both paths go along the coast of the Pacific Ocean for the most part – civilizations in each path "marching" in successive order. The discussion in Blaha (2010) was:

A Peruvian Sequence of Civilizations
Beginning as early as 2700 BC a series of civilizations developed along the coast of Ecuador, Peru and Chile. It appears that the first civilization was at Caral in the Supe River Valley about 120 miles north of Lima. The main features of the Caral civilization are described in subsection 6.1.1.

6.1.1 Caral Civilization: 2700? BC – 1800 BC – Norte Chico Region, Peru
The Caral archaeological site[35] is about 120 miles north of Lima, Peru in the Supe River Valley. This remarkable site has six enormous pyramids that date back to about 2627 BC making them older than the three great Egyptian pyramids at Giza. These pyramid complexes were built in stages starting around 2627 BC. The pyramid complexes were extended and rebuilt over the following 1000 years. Unlike the Egyptian pyramids which served as the tombs of pharaohs the pyramids and associated platforms and buildings served as ceremonial religious sites and governmental centers. The pyramids were the "center" of a densely populated area that was perhaps the first city in the Americas. The city grew food and cotton from irrigated agriculture in the Supe Valley, and traded cotton goods with fishermen on the coast for seafood and with Amazonian tribes for their products. (Cotton appears to have been grown in abundance in the Supe Valley.)

---

[35] I am grateful to Dr. Ruth Shady, discoverer of Caral and Director of the Anthropology Museum, San Marcos University in Lima, Peru for providing me with current information on Caral. My thanks also to Professor Winifred Creamer, Department of Anthropology, Northern Illinois University for information on the dating of the Caral pyramids.

One of the most amazing features of the Caral pyramid complex and civilization is the absence of fortifications. Apparently the *Caral civilization was a truly isolated civilization* and perhaps the only civilization in the Americas in the third millenium BC. Thus it may not have had significant enemies and little need for defensive structures.

In view of the civilizations that developed subsequently in the valleys of Peru (culminating in the Inca Empire) the Caral civilization may well be the "mother civilization" of the west coast of South America. As Professor Creamer pointed out, "This may actually be the birthplace of civilization in the Americas."

The six pyramids are arranged to form a huge public plaza. The largest pyramid called Piramide Mayor is 60 feet high and has a 450 by 500 foot base. These pyramids appear to have been built in a relatively short period of time in one or two phases. Thus one is led to believe that a large, skilled labor force was available for construction.

Recently a carving of the Staff god - a creature with fangs and splayed feet that holds a snake and a staff – was found on a bowl dated[36] to 2500 BC in Peru's Patavilca River Valley near Caral in Norte Chico. This bowl suggests that the Caral civilization had an organized religion.

By about 1800 BC the Caral area centers were largely abandoned. It appears that population groups moved both northward and southward carrying the seeds of the next generation of Peruvian civilizations with them. It is possible this migration was due to the exhaustion of the local soil and/or the availability of more fertile ground to the north and south.

As Dr. Jonathan Haas has pointed out[19] "The cultural pattern that emerged in this small area in the third millennium BC later established a foundation for 4,000 years of cultural florescence in other parts of the Andes." Dr. Creamer has remarked, "It is interesting that in the Casma valley, which is directly north, there are even bigger pyramids, and that was the next major cultural event."

The specification of the growth/Societal Level curve for Caral civilization is somewhat problematic. We know the approximate building point of the pyramids was 2627 BC and we know the civilization ended in approximately 1800 BC. Based on the Egyptian Giza pyramids case we will assume that the start of the building of the Caral pyramids was midway through the Startup period. Since the length of the Startup period is about 134 years we will assume the Startup time was 2627 + 67 = 2694 BC.

It is plotted in Fig. 7.1 together with the known historical data. The lack of historical data makes it difficult to assess the accuracy of the growth/Societal Level. However it is interesting that the Caral civilization gradually melted away towards the conclusion of the Universal State period.

---

[36] Haas, J., Creamer, W. & Ruiz, A., Archaeology (2003).

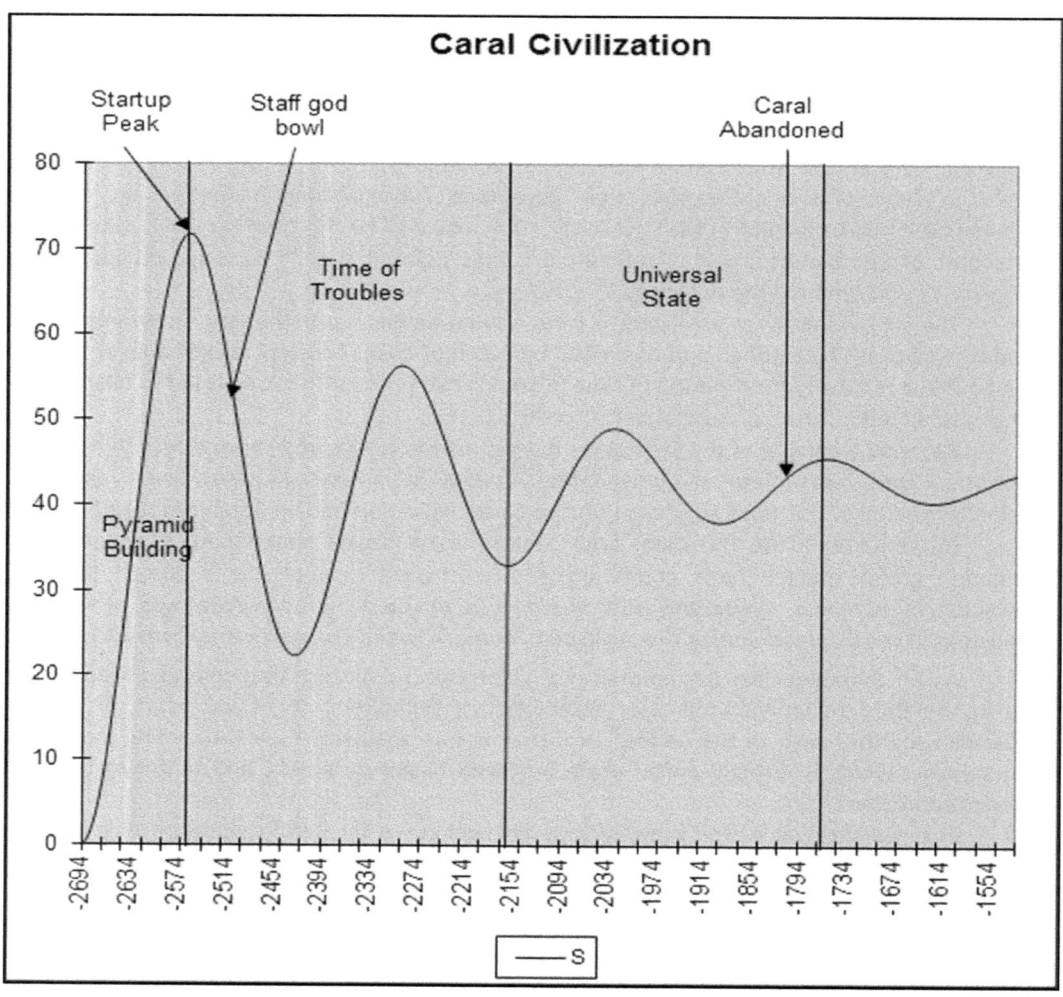

Table 7.1. Caral Peruvian Civilization Growth Curve.

The other sequence consists of Caral, La Florida, Huari, Chincha, and Inca civilizations. The latter three civilizations in this sequence are to the south of Lima. Cuzco, home of Inca civilization, is about 300 km southeast of Huari. Chincha is on the coast about 200 km from Huari. Huari is about 300 km from La Florida, and La Florida is about 200 km southeast of Caral.

The Tiwanaku civilization does not appear to be part of a sequence although traces of its artifacts were found at Huari and elsewhere in the Andes. It appears to have disappeared by 1200 AD. This civilization, which lasted from perhaps 200 BC to 1000 AD, dominated southern Peru, northern Chile, and eastern and southern Bolivia. Its capital city has an enormous step pyramid, the Akapana Pyramid. Most of its major buildings were constructed between 200 AD and 600 AD.

The two sequences of Peruvian civilizations that we have identified follow interesting geographic paths. Sequence I civilizations tend to go northward. Sequence II civilizations tend to go southward although the Inca civilization conquered both the northern and southern regions. The map in Fig. 7.3 graphically illustrates this point as does the distances between the various sites given above.

6.1.3 Sequence I of Peruvian Civilizations: Caral, Casma, Moche, Chimú

Between the Caral civilization (subsection 6.1.1) and Moche civilization (subsection 6.1.4) we find the Casma civilization. The Casma civilization appears to have been a successor civilization to Caral. As Caral melted away in the 19th century BC Casma civilization began and reached a Startup about 1500 BC. It ended in 400 BC. Little is known of its history although its monumental buildings and artifacts are still the subject of continuing study.

The successor of Casma civilization was Moche civilization (considered in the next subsection.) This civilization lasted from about 400 BC to 750 AD.

The successor of Moche civilization was Chimú civilization which lasted from about 1000 AD to 1460 AD. Chimú civilization also started in the Moche River Valley. Its capital was Chan Chan. In 1370 AD the Chimú ruler Ñançen Pinco expanded Chimú to include the territory from the Saña River in the north to the Santa River in the south. In the 15th century until the 1460's Minchan Çaman expanded the domain further north to Piura and south to Lima. We estimate a Startup for Chimú by assuming 1370 is the beginning of its Universal State and thus the Startup is 1370 − 400 − 134 = 836 AD. Chimú was conquered in the 1460's by the Incas. Fig. 6.4 shows our curve of the growth/Societal Level $S_{Peruvian I}$ based on these startups.

6.1.4 Moche (Mochica) Civilization, Northern Peru: 400 BC? – 750 AD

The city of Moche in the Moche Valley is the site of two large structures: the Temple of the Sun (a step pyramid) and the Temple of the Moon (a giant terraced platform). At its greatest extent the civilization extended approximately 350 km along the coast of northern Peru from the Nepeña River Valley northwards to the Lambayeque River Valley. The Startup point of this civilization is unclear. However the giant Moche structures seem to have been constructed starting from about 0 AD. In addition many richly furnished burial chambers containing sophisticated jewelry and other artifacts date to the period around 300 AD. (See Davies (1997).)

The Moche civilization was dealt an almost fatal blow – a climatic catastrophe – in the period from 550 AD – 600 AD: a 30 year period of rains and floods (a mega El Niño) followed by a 30+ year period of drought.[37] The remnants of the civilization continued to exist for another 150 years to about 750 AD. However their buildings changed from huacas (pyramidal structures)

---

[37] Dr Lonnie Thompson, Climatologist, Ohio State University.

prior to the climatic catastrophe to fortresses. Apparently central authority broke down and the civilization split into warring communities competing for food and other scarce resources.[38]

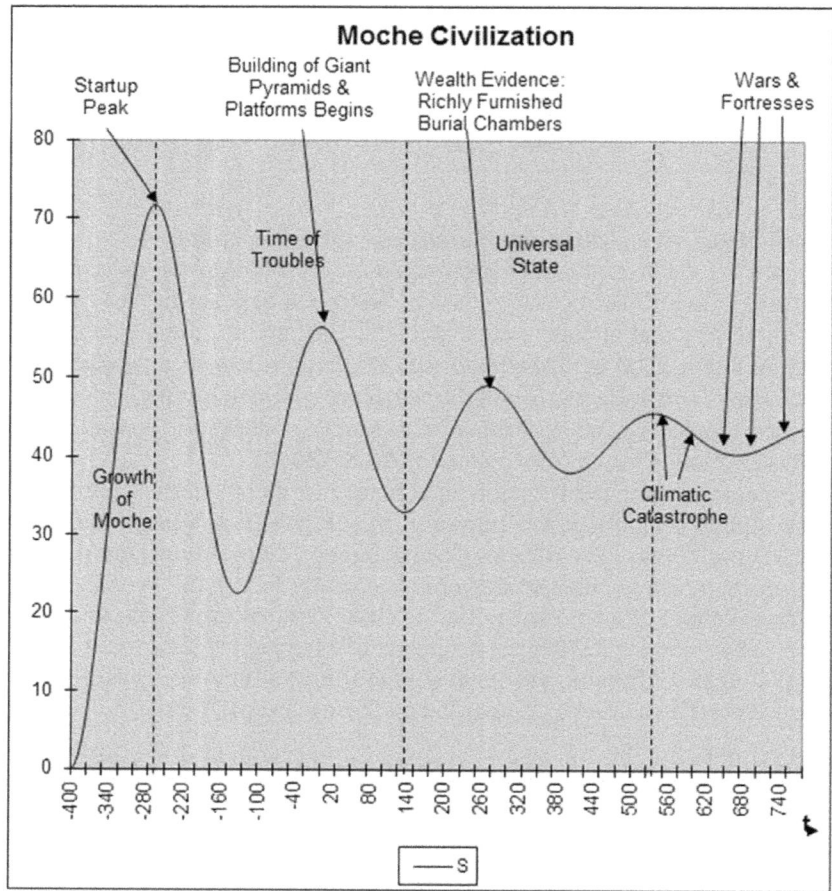

Figure 7.2. The Growth/Societal Level of Moche civilization compared to known events in Moche history.

Fig.7.2 plots and displays the known facts of Moche civilization which correlate amazingly well with the peaks and valleys of the growth/Societal Level:

- A Startup around 400 BC.
- The beginning of pyramid and giant platform building around 0 AD – a peak.
- A period of prosperity as evidenced by richly furnished tombs around 300 AD – a peak.
- A climatic catastrophe between 550 AD and 600 AD – a rout.

---

[38] Dr Tom D. Dillehay, Dept. of Anthropology, Vanderbilt Univ. in Pillsbury (2006).

- A period of warfare after the climatic catastrophe lasting to about 750 AD – a valley.

6.1.5 Sequence II of Peruvian Civilizations: Caral, La Florida, Huari, Chincha, Inca

Sequence II of the Peruvian civilizations also appears to have begun in Caral – the "mother" of Peruvian civilizations. When Caral dissolved towards 1800 BC it appears that its people dispersed both to the north and to the south.

The Casma civilization nicely fills the period from 1500 BC to 400 BC in the north. The successor of the Caral civilization in the south is problematic. We know that a huge pyramid and large building complex appeared in La Florida in the period from 1710 BC to perhaps 776 BC. We also know that successor civilizations generally seem to appear 200 – 300 km from their parent civilization in both sequence I and sequence II. The Lima – La Florida region is about 200 km southeast of Caral. Thus the time period, and the distance, seems appropriate for a civilization at La Florida. However the building complex at La Florida is largely unexplored and the extent of this civilization is unknown. Thus we will simply assume it existed as an intermediate civilization in sequence II (pending archaeological verification.)

The Huari civilization in the central Peruvian Highlands lasted from about 200 BC to 1000 AD. The first period of the settlement of Huari occupied the period from 200 BC to 600 AD. A sizeable Huari empire existed from 600 AD to 1000 AD from Cajamarca and the Chicama Valley in the north to the Ocoña Valley on the south – a distance of approximately 1000 km. The Huari city fell in 800 AD at the empire's peak, and the remainder of their domain slowly was lost over the following 200 years.

The successor of the Huari civilization appears to be the Chincha civilization (c. 1000 AD – 1450 AD) on the southern coast of Peru. This civilization was oriented to the sea and is said to have had large fleets of fishing vessels (in the thousands) that traveled to the fish-laden waters of northern Peru beyond the reach of the cold Antarctic current. At the time of the Spanish Conquest, Chincha was listed as having 30,000 households. We estimate a Startup for Chincha civilization at 1000 – 134 = 866 AD.

Inca civilization appears to have started in the 14th century. (The thought arises that we see here a parallel to Hellenic civilization with seafaring Greeks in the beginning and the Roman Empire as the Universal State.) In 1432 the Incas were confined to villages in the Cuzco Valley. The Incas record nine early rulers before Pachakuti 'Inka who reigned from 1438 to 1471 AD. Pachakuti and his successor Thupa 'Inka (who reigned from 1471 to 1493 AD) completed the expansion of the Inca Empire, which began in the 14th century under the fourth emperor Mayta Capac.

From 1493 – 1532 two wars of succession occurred. Thus when the Spanish arrived in 1532 they were able to take advantage of the opposing sides of the supporters of Huascar and Atahuallpa to conquer the Inca Empire. We assume the beginning of the civil war in 1493 is the Startup peak (Breakdown) and thus the Inca Startup is 1493 – 134 = 1359 AD.

Based on this limited information we can construct a growth/Societal Level curve for this sequence of civilizations (Fig. 7.4).

© S. Blaha 2014 All Rights Reserved.

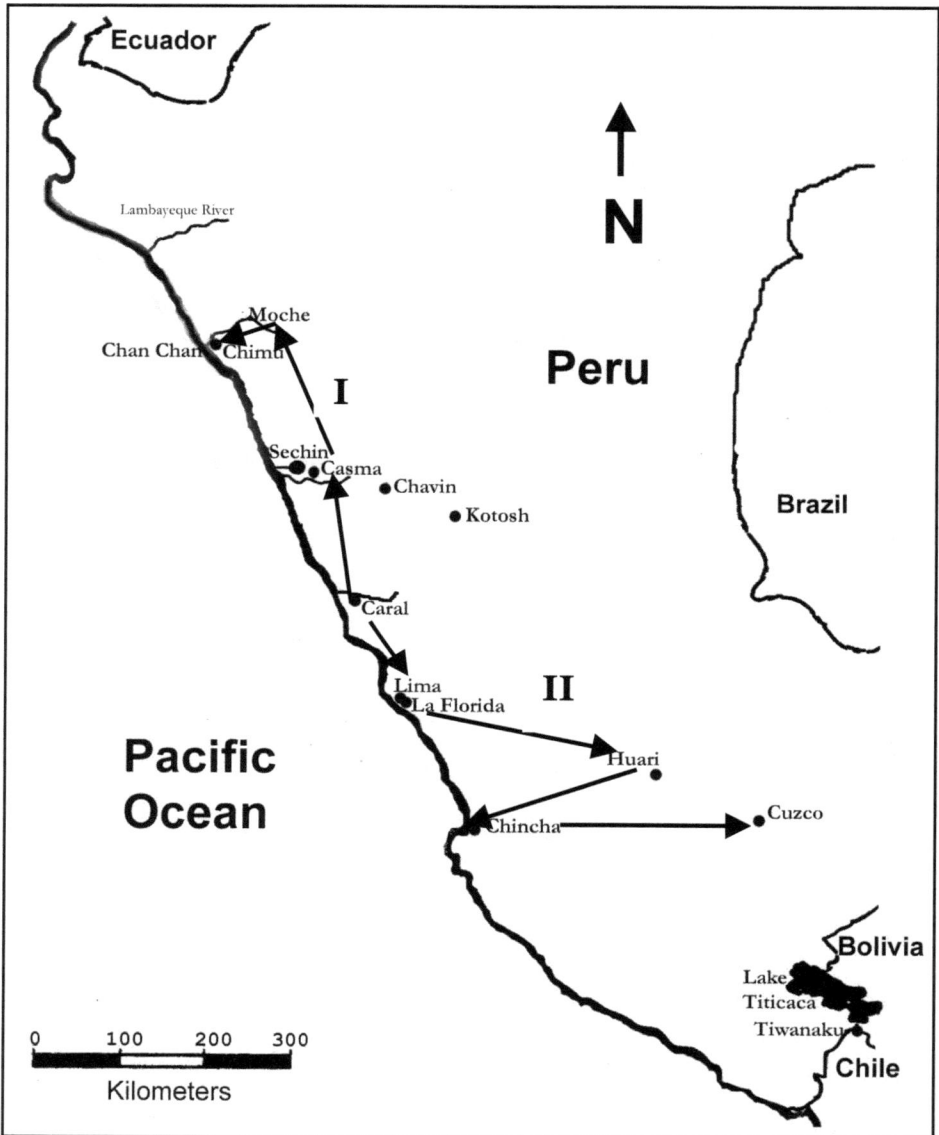

Figure 7.3. Two sequences of civilizations: sequence I goes generally north from Caral; sequence II goes generally south from Caral. The Inca civilization grew from Cuzco to absorb all of the coast and highlands between northern Chile and Ecuador.

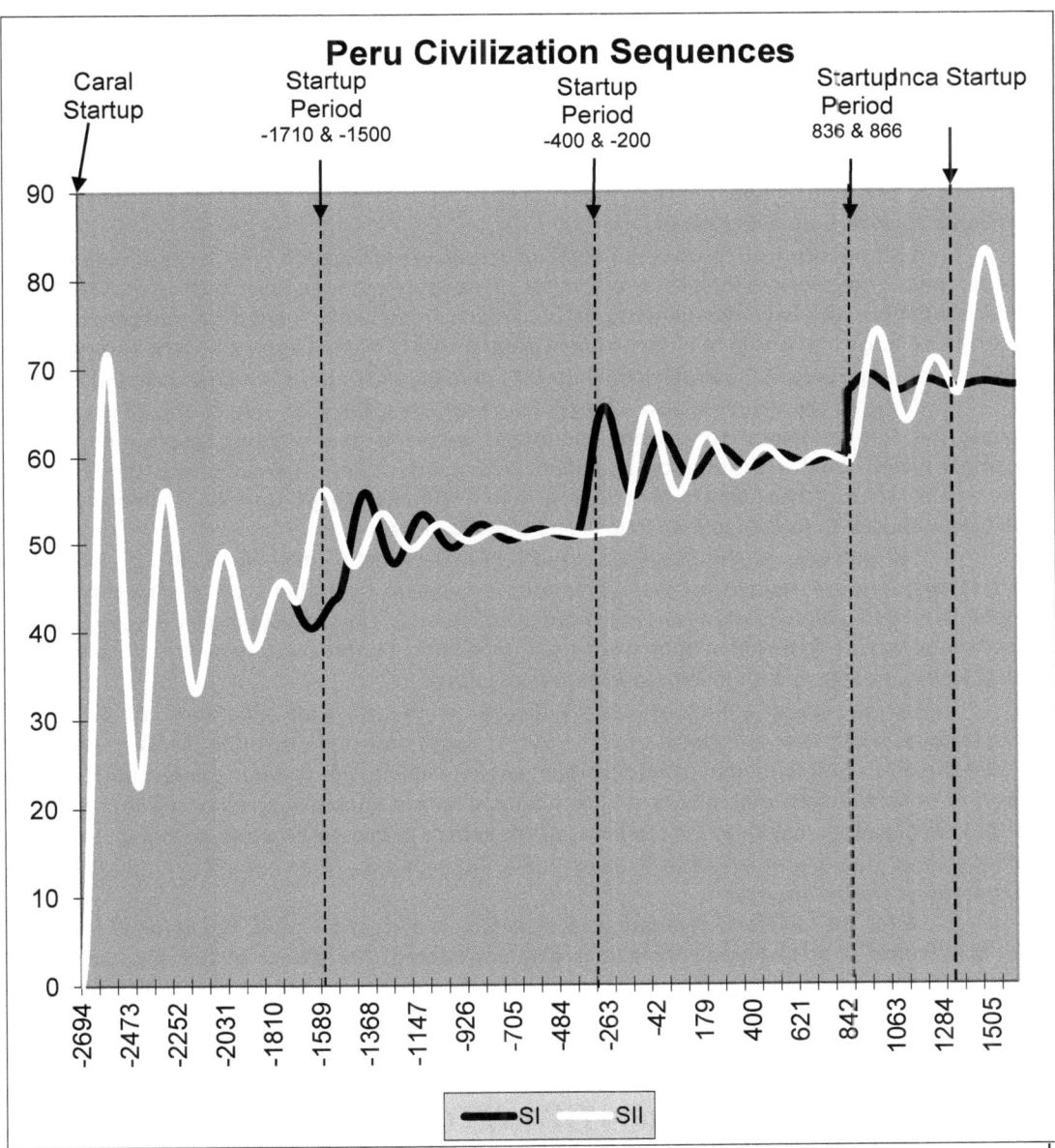

Figure 7.4. The growth/Societal Levels of the sequences: Caral, Casma, Moche and Chimú civilizations (black line labeled SI); and Caral, La Florida, Huari, Chincha, and Inca civilizations (white line labeled SII).

6.1.6 Observations on Andean Geography

The coastal and highland areas of Peru offer a unique *linear* geography for the development and spread of civilization. If Caral is indeed the mother of Peruvian civilizations, as its age and central location (on the Peruvian coast) suggest, then we see sequences I and II represent the successive flowering and expansion of successor civilizations in a remarkably orderly fashion to the north, and to the south, resulting eventually in a unified Inca state embracing the entire region. *In this respect one is reminded of the growth of ant colonies and microbe colonies – superorganisms.*

A comparison of the development of Peruvian civilizations with its one dimensional geographic framework with the development of civilizations elsewhere such as in China and Mesopotamia which have two-dimensional geographic frameworks suggest the complexity of the succession of civilizations in two-dimensional geographies is due in large part to the geography. A two-dimensional geography enables the interplay of many civilizations in a checkerboard fashion.

Egyptian civilization is also a long linear area along the Nile. Due to the ease of travel along the Nile compared to crossing mountains between river valleys, Egypt underwent a comparatively rapid transition to a unified civilization rather than following the Peruvian sequences to the Inca, which took almost four millennia. Egypt was also somewhat two-dimensional due to its contacts with Libya and the Middle East.

The similarity of the sequence I and II growth/Societal Level curves in Fig. 7.4 is also interesting because sequence I was dominated by coastal civilizations while sequence II was dominated by highland civilizations (with some exceptions). The almost parallel development of both sequences suggests that they were both dominated by the cyclic behavior of civilizations that we have suggested is universal and genetically based.

An interesting aspect of each sequence is the physical separation of successive civilizations, which was a distance of 200 – 300 km with only one exception (Moche → Chimú). Since the only mode of human transportation was by walking, this distance represented 20 – 30 days of travel between civilizations at 10 km per day for mountainous travel by armies. Thus 200 – 300 km distances may relate to the limits of the sphere of control of armies although the Huari domain was 1000 km in length at its peak in 800 AD. However, the reason for a 200 – 300 km separation remains uncertain.

Lastly, the La Florida civilization remains largely a question mark. The pyramid and large building complex at La Florida remains largely unexplored. The extent of the population that supported its construction, and the history of this population, as well as its political constitution as city-states and/or an empire, are also unknowns. Its location, and the gap it fills in sequence II, argues for its existence. But decisive archaeological data is not available as yet.

7.1 New Data on the Huari (Wari) Civilization

The Huari or Wari civilization covered much of Peru. A detailed study of the thousands of archaeological sites by R. Alan Covey et al[39] shows it consisted of colonies spread over much of Peru. The Wari were oriented towards trade and

---

[39] Journal of Anthropological Archaeology, October, 2013 issue.

colonization. Their semiautonomous colonies formed a patchwork quilt and were part of a web of trading routes. The Wari (Huari) empire lasted from about 600 AD to 1000 AD (a four hundred year Universal State period as predicted by our theory) as suggested in the previous part of this chapter. The Wari civilization lasted from 200 AD to 1000 AD with the first four hundred years (200 AD to 600 AD) being a "Time of Troubles." There was a 134 year Startup period prior to the Time of Troubles during which the Wari grew to statehood based on their capital city of Pikillacta. The Startup period has not been documented although a period of growth is undoubtedly required for the Wari to reach major status.

8. New Data for Anatolian Civilizations

8.1 Theory Applied to Early Anatolian Civilizations

In Blaha (2010) and earlier books we applied our theory to very early Anatolian civilizations. In our view a civilization may have a small population of the order of 5,000 inhabitants although we most often think of civilizations as composed of many hundreds of thousands or millions. This premise is based on the known physical principle that relatively small numbers can show statistical (thermodynamic) behavior. Our theory is based on energetic (thermodynamic) principles.

Part of our discussion of Early Anatolian civilizations, which admittedly have small populations of the order of 5000 to 10,000 people, is the following passages from Blaha (2010):

A Prehistoric Anatolian Sequence of Civilizations
At the beginning of this chapter we pointed out an apparent similarity between Caral in Peru and Çatalhöyük in Turkey. In view of the sequences of civilizations that we have found in Peru it seems reasonable to inquire whether a sequence(s) of civilizations can be found in Anatolia.

Anatolia does not have a linear geography like coastal Peru. Therefore we can expect the sequence(s) of civilizations to show a two-dimensional "fan-out" and thus be less obvious. Fig. 6.8 shows some early civilizations/societies in Anatolia. Some of these civilizations/societies extend back in time to approximately 9400 BC – before the relatively warm, stable climate that arrived around 8000 BC marking the beginning of the Neolithic Period.

In the period from 9,600 BC to 8,000 BC the earth appears to have warmed by about 19° C or about 1.2° C per century. (Compare this warming rate to global warming today which amounted to about ½° C in the past century.) During this warming period, starting perhaps as early as the beginning of warming 9,600 BC, significant communities and religious centers began to appear. **The Göbekli Tepe ceremonial center in southeastern Turkey appeared by 9,300 BC. It has colossal, carved columns and sizeable monumental structures.** Jerico (Tall As-Sultãn) appeared by 9,000 BC. At Aşikli Höyük a town of hunter-gatherers appeared by 8,400 BC with perhaps a few thousand inhabitants. The town has residential buildings and some streets but no obvious fortifications.

Figure 6.8. Early civilizations/societies in Neolithic, and Preneolithic, Anatolia.

    Starting about 9,000 BC we see the beginnings of agricultural cultivation and animal domestication in the Fertile Crescent. And then in 8,000 BC after "global warming" is over the Neolithic Period proper begins. Farming, and villages, are firmly established in the Tigris and Euphrates Valleys, and in Syria, Lebanon, Israel and Jordan, before 7,000 BC and in Greece by 7,000 BC. The Neolithic Period starts in the Indus River Valley by 5,000 BC, in Southeast Asia and the Yellow River Valley (China) by 3,500 BC, and in Mexico and Central America by 6,500 BC.

    A series of settlements appeared across Anatolia within this framework of Neolithic hunter-gatherer groups and small agricultural communities that were interconnected through widespread trading channels (which also promoted information exchange). These settlements were the intermediaries that eventually brought Neolithic culture to Europe Some of these settlements are shown on the map in Fig. 6.8 and listed in Table 6.2.

© S. Blaha 2014 All Rights Reserved.

Name	Approximate Dates	Artifacts	Structures	Fortifications
Göbekli Tepe Ceremonial Center?	9560 BC – 8430 BC (radiocarbon dates)	None?	7 m. tall, Colossal (50 ton) Carved pillars, Monuments	None
Aşikli Höyük Hunter-Gatherers?	8400 BC – 7500 BC	No, Animal figurines, Beads	Residences, Streets, buildings	None
Pinarbaşi	Pre-Çatalhöyük layers; 750 – 1300 years earlier than Çatalhöyük	Yes	Yes	None
Kaltepe	Pre-Çatalhöyük quarry 400 – 1020 years earlier than Çatalhöyük	Yes	Quarry	None
Can Hasan	Layers 750 – 1300 years earlier than Çatalhöyük	Yes	Yes	None
Hacilar	Layers 100 – 970 years earlier than Çatalhöyük; also 5600 BC – 5200 BC	goddess figures	Yes	None
Pre-Pottery Neolithic B Abu Hureyra	7300? BC – 5800 BC	beads	Residences	?
Çatalhöyük	7500 BC – 6000 BC	Yes	Residences, no streets	None?

Table 6.2. A table of some Neolithic and Chalcolithic civilizations. A number of others are not listed including Musular and Suberde. The dates for the Pre-Çatalhöyük layers are the "most likely" estimates from Hodder (2006) and are subject to change.

Origin of Çatalhöyük

Çatalhöyük stands out amongst these sites because of its size in the 7th millennium BC. It appears to have had a population of between 5,000 – 7,000 persons in its prime and consisted of roughly 900 buildings. The only comparable city in that period in the Near East was Abu Hureyra[40] in Syria. Because of Çatalhöyük's population and the length of its existence (over a

---

[40] Abu Hureyra, a site on the Euphrates River in Northern Syria. was occupied in several phases: one phase of occupation occurred in the 9th millennium BC. Then after a long unoccupied period it was reoccupied (by a Pre-Pottery Neolithic B culture) in the 7th millennium – probably after a warmer spell that began around

thousand years) we identify it as a civilization and believe it to be comparable to Caral in Peru (which had a similar population and lifetime.)

The origin of Çatalhöyük is uncertain but an interesting survey by Baird[41] of a 1,000 square kilometer area around Çatalhöyük revealed that settlements existed within the survey area since about 17,000 BC. In particular, in the 8th millennium there were 4 – 6 small settlements in the area. By 7,000 BC these settlements appear to have disappeared and only Çatalhöyük exists. In Baird's view the population of these settlements was most likely absorbed by the much larger Çatalhöyük. It is possible that they went to Çatalhöyük for reasons of safety (safety in numbers), or to take advantage of the division of labor that accompanies a larger population (stonesmiths, more varied diets due to more farming activity, more social/religious life.) While Çatalhöyük does not have obvious fortifications, the continuous outer wall of a community without streets could play the role of a defensive wall. If attacked the population could bombard the invaders with rocks from their rooftops. It is interesting that an earlier site of hunter-gatherers, Aşikli Höyük, had buildings that were separated by streets in some cases. Based on this fact, the continuous outer wall of Çatalhöyük takes on more significance. The first appearance of true defensive walls (with slits) was at nearby Mersin in 5200 BC – well after the occupation of Çatalhöyük.

The reason for the settlement of Çatalhöyük is uncertain, as is the reason for its demise.

A Sequence of Anatolian Civilizations

An examination of Fig. 6.8 and Table 6.2 reveals an apparent sequence of civilizations. However it is clear that this sequence in the Neolithic and Chalcolithic periods is sequential within a common cultural milieu that seems to have been bonded by the sinews of trade and the travels of nomadic hunter-gatherer groups. Thus we see a westward moving sequence of civilizations:

Abu Hureyra	$10^{th} – 9^{th}$ Millenium BC
Göbekli Tepe	9560 BC – 8430 BC
Aşikli Höyük	8400 BC – 7500 BC
Çatalhöyük	7500 BC – 6000 BC
Hacilar	5600 BC – 5200 BC

based on the broad range of cultural/trade connections in the region. This sequence invites comparison to the Peruvian sequences that we examined in the previous section.

7500 BC. It achieved large size (about 37 acres) – larger than Çatalhöyük (32 acres), and then was abandoned about 5800 BC.

[41] D. Baird, "Konya Plain Survey", Anatolian Archaeology **7**, 16 (2001).

8.2 New Data[42] on Göbekli Tepe – One of the Earliest Known Civilized Sites

Göbekli Tepe is the world's oldest monumental temple. It appears to have been built to observe and perhaps worship Sirius, known as the Dog Star. It consists of twenty circular areas – each surrounded by massive columns of a size comparable to the columns in Egyptian temples. It is unique because it was constructed by hunter-gatherer settlements who were a civilization of sorts as indicated by the massive construction efforts needed to build the temple. Thus it shows that agriculture, which is not present in the vicinity of the temple, is not a prerequisite for a civilization. A civilization can be built on the energetics of superlative hunter-gatherer activity that enables a population to develop the trappings of civilization.

There appears to be evidence that the temple was built to observe Sirius, a bright star that was often of interest in early times. Giulio Magli of the Polytechnic University of Milan studied the alignments of three of the excavated rings. These appear to be aligned with the points on the horizon where Sirius would have risen in 9100 BC, 8750 BC and 8300 BC. Sirius first became visible above the horizon due to the wobble of the earth's axis in 9300 BC which is consistent with the dating of the beginning of construction of the temple as noted in the previous section.

If the astronomical view of the temple's structure is correct, then we have clear evidence of a civilizational activity: astronomy, and of the ability of a people to engage in monumental construction. Together these clues strongly favor the existence of civilizations at the dawn of the present era of good climate[43] which started in 10,000 BC. One can wonder if other civilizations of that era existed and are yet to be found. One can also wonder at the rapid transition to civilizations after the world climate ameliorated. We list candidate civilizations in Table 6.2 in section 8.1 above.

---

[42] Giulio Magli, arXiv:1307.8397 (2013).
[43] Warm temperatures without massive up and down temperature spikes. Preceding millennia had frequent major changes in world temperature.

9. New Data for Early Egyptian Civilization

In our earlier books we proposed the existence of an Egyptian civilization, that we called Nile River Civilization, which predated the classical Egyptian civilization that built the great pyramids.

9.1 Early Egyptian Civilization
The following discussion appeared in Blaha (2010) and his earlier books:

9.1.2 Nile River Civilization: 3691 BC – 2690 BC
Both the Egyptaic and the Sinic civilizations have writings referring to an earlier stage in their civilizations, or a predecessor civilization, that existed prior to the known civilizations with which we are familiar. These periods were more or less prior to the development of writing in the respective civilizations.

Some Egyptian and Greek historical records describe a period of civilization with a united Egypt under the Pharaoh Menes in 3000 BC. While we often think of Egyptaic civilization as suddenly flowering from nothing, and then immediately building pyramids, there is a long prior period during which the Nile Valley was brought into cultivation, and societies and governments developed. This prior period encompassed the 0th and 1st Dynasties. It included the legendary kings:

Ka
Narmer
Aha
Djer
Djet
Den
Anedjub
Semerkhet
Qa'a

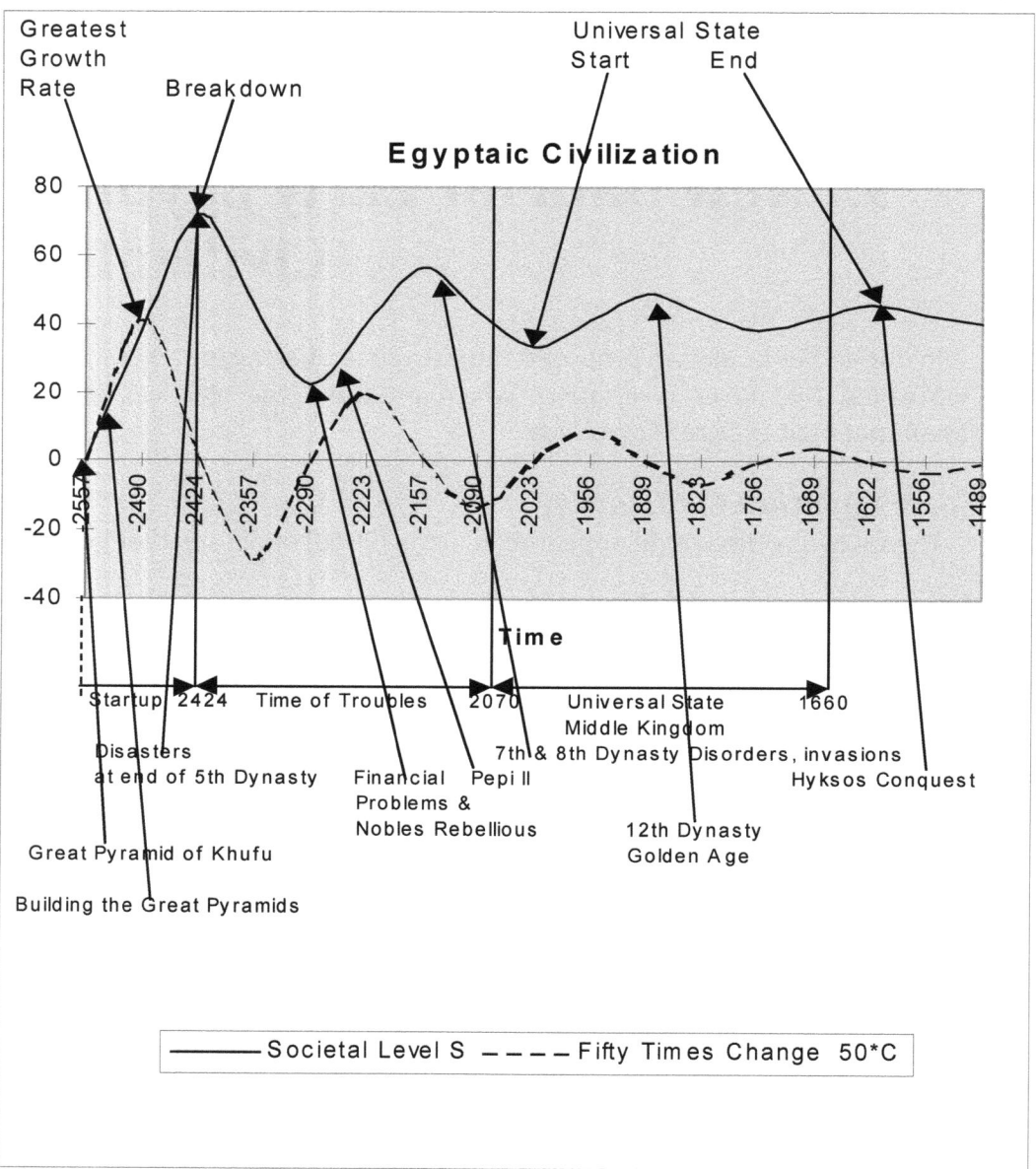

Figure 9.1. Plot of growth/Societal Level S(t) (and the growth change function C(t) multiplied by fifty) for Egyptian civilization with historical events marked on the graph (from Blaha (2002).) The growth/Societal Level curve (eq. 8.9) is in good overall agreement with the trends of events.

King Narmer appears to be the King who united Upper and Lower Egypt based primarily on a shield-shaped sculpture called the Narmer Palette that has been dated to 3150 – 3125 BC. The front side of the Narmer Palette shows Narmer wearing the White Crown of Upper Egypt in the act of striking an enemy from the marshlands. The rear side shows Narmer wearing the Red Crown of Lower Egypt (the Nile delta) as he inspects the bodies of headless enemies.

In the period from 3500 BC to 2600 BC, Egypt evolved from two separate regions, Upper Egypt with strong African influences and Lower Egypt (the Nile delta region) with strong Libyan and Middle Eastern influences, into one unified kingdom. The building of the great pyramids that followed reflected the wealth and power of a united Egypt. This later Egypt was the Egypt of Egyptaic civilization.

But the prior one thousand years contained an Egypt of various states created during and after the taming of the Nile Valley. It also developed a universal state that existed for about four hundred years before the beginning of Egyptaic civilization (which we have set for good reason at 2557 BC.)

The only other important "known facts" of the thousand years of prehistory are:

- A major (unspecified) calamity took place in the reign of King Semerkhet around 2800 BC,
- An upheaval appears to have happened during the reign of King Qa'a,
- A major rivalry existed between the cults of Set and Horus around 2725 BC.

Although the data on Egyptian prehistory is somewhat sketchy we can use our theory of civilizations to develop a picture of that civilization based on any one of the following dates:

1. The beginning of the time of troubles
2. The end of the time of troubles
3. The beginning of a universal state
4. The end of a universal state

Any one of these data items fixes the growth curve S for the civilization. Any other information that we have on the civilization can then be used to check the routs and rallies of the S curve to confirm its validity.[44]

The Narmer palette showing Narmer wearing the White Crown of Upper Egypt and the Red Crown of Lower Egypt is believed to indicate that Narmer united Upper and Lower Egypt into a universal state. Other historical data indicates his central importance. Since the Narmer Palette

---

[44] Similarly we can examine the information in early Chinese writings referring to prehistoric dynasties and empires from the period before the recognized beginning of Sinic civilization. Again only one date is necessary to fix the S growth curve for a possible pre-Sinic civilization.

has been dated to 3150 – 3125 BC we have chosen 3157 BC as the beginning of the universal state of a prehistoric civilization that we will call *Nile River civilization*.

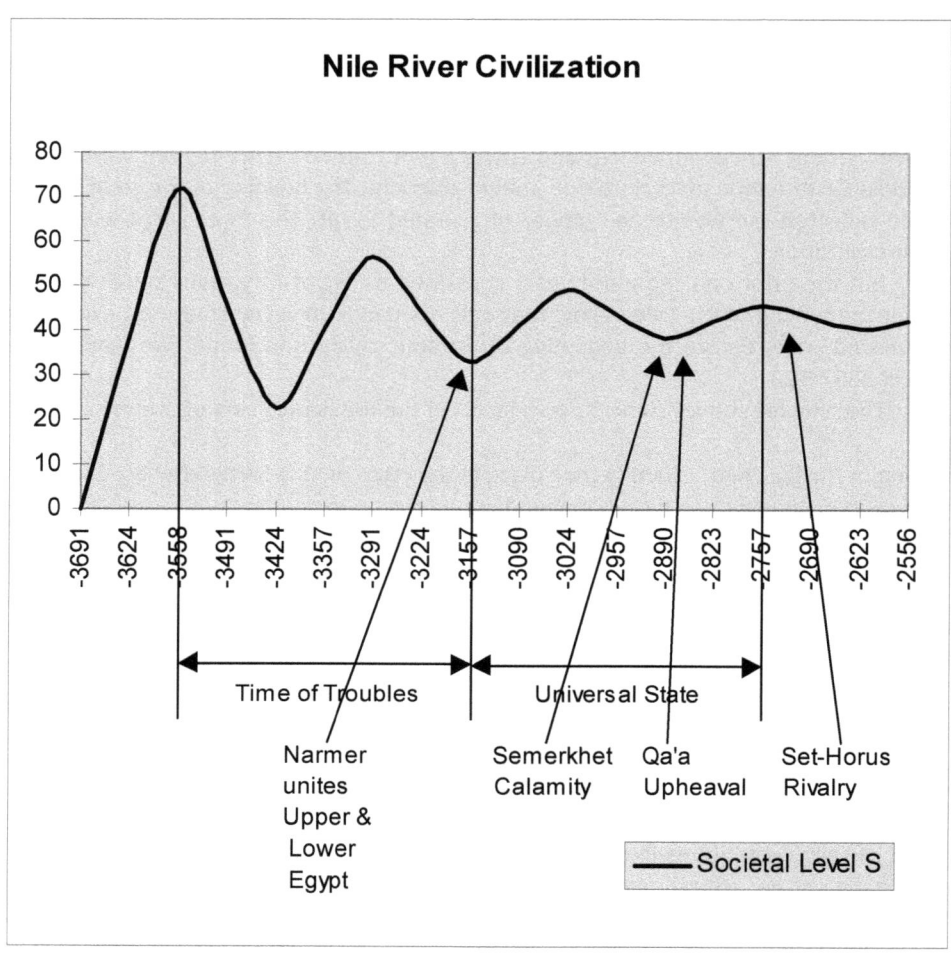

Figure 9.2. Growth/Societal Level curve of proposed Nile River civilization.

Allotting 400 years for a time of troubles and 134 years for a Startup phase we arrive at a beginning date of Nile River civilization of 3691 BC. We use the standard theory of a civilization to obtain the growth/Societal curve shown in Figure 9.2.

The Semerkhet Calamity and the Qa'a Upheaval appear at a low point of the theoretical growth/Societal Level. Also, the rivalry between the Set and Horus cults appears on the slope of a downturn in the growth/Societal Level. Thus there is a correlation between known historical events, and the routs and rallies of the growth/Societal curve. As further archaeological data surfaces, more detailed tests of the S curve of the Nile River civilization will be possible.

The complete growth/Societal curve of the sequence of Egyptian civilizations is given in Fig. 9.3.

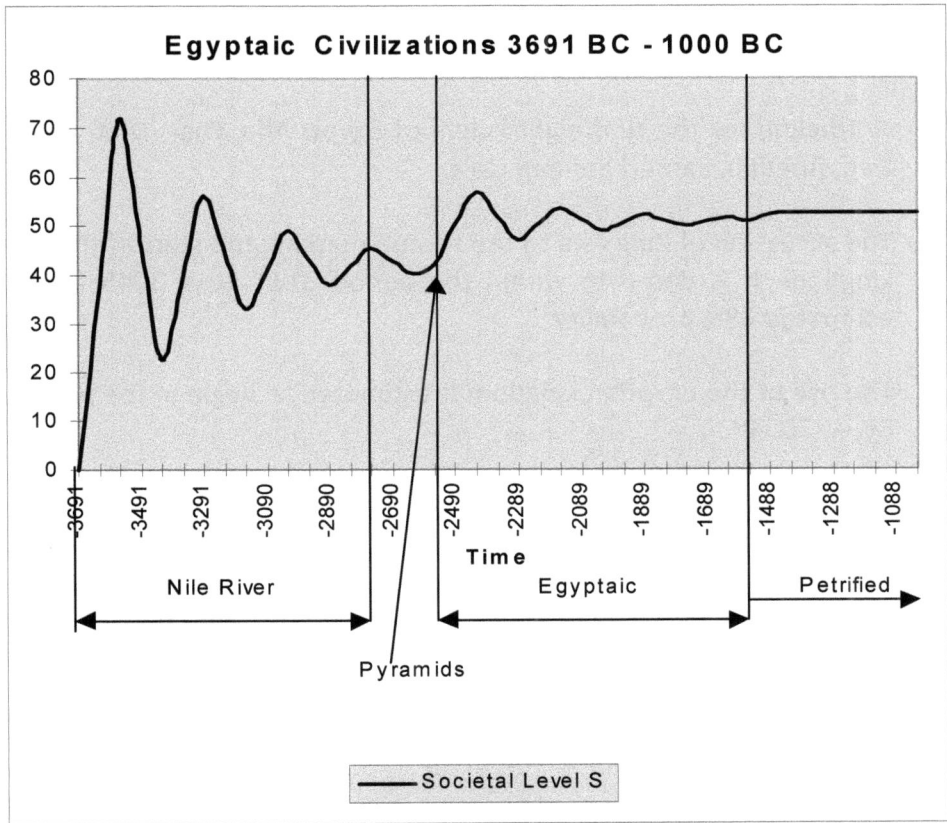

Figure 9.3. The Nile River and Egyptaic civilizations 3691 BC – 1000 BC growth/Societal Level curve S.

9.2 New Data on Early Egyptian (Nile River) Civilization - Rulers

Recently new data has appeared from a team of Oxford University archaeologists[45] that radiocarbon dated organic parts of artifacts and animal remains in stored museum vaults and then computer analyzed the obtained dates to narrow the radiocarbon dates to within 32 years with 68% probability. The new data yielded:

1. A timeline for the first eight rulers of Egypt: Aha, Djer, Djet, Merneith, Den, Anedjib, Semerkhet and Qa'a.

2. The accession of King Aha to the throne marking the start of the Egyptian kingdom. It is dated to within the period 3111 BC – 3045 BC with an estimated 68% probability.

3. The rise of the Egyptian kingdom is estimated to begin in the period 3800 BC – 3700 BC.

4. With a 68% probability the dates of rule of the first rulers are (to within 32 years): King Djer (3073 BC–3036 BC), King Djet (2989 BC–2941 BC), Queen Merneith (2946 BC–2916 BC), King Den (2928 BC–2911 BC), King Anedjib (2916 BC–2896 BC), King Semerkhet (2912 BC–2891 BC), and King Qa'a (2906 BC–2886 BC).

If we compare the above findings with our analysis we find:

1. Queen Merneith is omitted from our list – possibly because she was not male.

2. If we compare this new data with our chronology (Fig. 9.2 and the Narmer discussion) we find our suggested unification of Egypt in 3167 is close to the proposed range of dates in point 2 above after taking account of their 32 year accuracy range. Their choice of Aha as the first

---

[45] Michael Dee et al, Proceedings of the Royal Society A (September 4, 2013).

ruler of a unified Egypt seems inconsistent with the Narmer Palate although Aha certainly inherited a unified Egypt.

3. According to Fig. 9.2 above we estimated the Nile River civilization began in 3691 BC. This date is very consistent with the date range of 3800 BC – 3700 BC in point 3 above taking account of its 32 year accuracy range.

4. The dates of King Semerkhet (2912 BC–2891 BC), and King Qa'a (2906 BC–2886 BC) in point 4 above are consistent with our Fig. 9.2 above and the events of those years as exemplified by the growth curve in Fig. 9.2.

We conclude that this new archaeological data on early Egypt is consistent with our theory of the Nile River civilization presented in our earlier books.

9.3 New Data on Early Egyptian (Nile River) Civilization – Mummification

We have placed the origin of the Nile River civilization at 3691 BC (Fig. 9.2 above). For many years it was generally thought that formal mummification began around 2500 BC. Before that period it was thought that mummification was done naturally by placing wrapped bodies in the dry desert air to mummify.

Recently, mummies dating to 4500 BC – 3350 BC have been found to have been mummified using "artificial" ingredients including plant oils, animal fats, resins, petroleum and aromatic antibacterial chemicals.[46] The recipe for making the mummifying fluid was quite similar in all the mummies from this period studied. In addition it was essentially the same recipe as that used in the Egyptaic civilization of the pyramids.

Given the importance of death and preparing the dead for the afterlife we conclude that Nile River civilization practiced largely the same death procedures as the following Egyptaic civilization. Thus we find further support for the existence of Nile River civilization and its continuity with the succeeding Egyptaic civilization, which has until our recent work, been largely viewed as the only Egyptian civilization.

---

[46] Jana Jones et al, PLoS ONE, 10.1371/journal.pone.0103608

9.4 Support for Nile River Civilization

The preceding new data strongly supports the existence of the Nile River civilization that we have proposed in earlier books. The civilization was fragmented into kingdoms in its early phase and later unified into a Universal State.

REFERENCES

Balter, M. 2005. *The Goddess and the Bull.* Simon & Schuster. New York.

Bernal, J. D. 1929. *The World, the Flesh and the Devil.* Indiana University Press. Bloomington, IN.

Blaha, S. 2002a. *The Rhythms of History: A Universal Theory of Civilizations.* Pingree-Hill Publishing. Auburn, NH.

_____. 2002b. *The Life Cycle of Civilizations.* Pingree-Hill Publishing. Auburn, NH.

_____. 2004a. *A Unified Quantitative Theory Of Civilizations and Societies: 9600 BC - 2100 AD.* Pingree-Hill Publishing. Auburn, NH.

_____. 2004b. *Quantum Big Bang Cosmology: Complex Space-time General Relativity, Quantum Coordinates, Dodecahedral Universe, Inflation, and New Spin 0, ½, 1 & 2 Tachyons & Imagyons.* Pingree-Hill Publishing. Auburn, NH.

_____. 2008. *A Complete Derivation of the Form of the Standard Model With a New Method to Generate Particle Masses: Second Edition.* Pingree-Hill Publishing. Auburn, NH.

_____. 2009a. *Bright Stars, Bright Universe: Advancing Civilization by Colonization Of The Solar System And The Stars Using A Fast Quark Drive.* Pingree-Hill Publishing. Auburn, NH.

_____. 2009b. *To Far Stars and Galaxies: Second Edition of Bright Stars, Bright Universe.* Pingree-Hill Publishing. Auburn, NH.

_____. 2010. *SuperCivilizations: Civilizations as Superorganisms.* McMann-Fisher Publishing, Auburn, NH.

_____, 2011b, *All the Universe! Faster Than Light Tachyon Quark Starships & Particle Accelerators with the LHC as a Prototype Starship Drive Scientific Edition* (Pingree-Hill Publishing, Auburn, NH, 2011).

_____, 2013a, *Multi-Stage Space Guns, Micro-Pulse Nuclear Rockets, and Faster-Than-Light Quark-Gluon Ion Drive Starships* (Blaha Research, Auburn, NH, 2013).

_____, 2014b, *All the Multiverse! Starships Exploring the Endless Universes of the Cosmos using the Baryonic Force* (Blaha Research, Auburn, NH, 2014)

_____, 2014c, *All the Multiverse! II Between Multiverse Universes* (Blaha Research, Auburn, NH, 2014)

Braudel, F. 1993. *A History of Civilizations.* Penguin Books. New York, NY.

Coulborn, R. 1969. *The Origin of Civilized Societies.* Princeton University Press. Princeton, NJ.

Davies, N. 1997. *The Ancient Kingdoms of Peru.* Penguin Books. London.

Feynman, R. P., Hibbs, A. R. and Styer, D. F. 2010. *Quantum Mechanics and Path Integrals: Emended Edition.* Dover. New York.

Gazlake, P. S. 1973. *Great Zimbabwe.* Hazell, Watson and Viney Ltd. Alesbury, United Kingdom.

Hesiod, (Tr. H. G. Evelyn-White). 1982. *Hesiod: The Homeric Hymns and Homerica..* Harvard University Press. Cambridge, MS, USA.

Strauss, W. and Howe, N. 1991. *Generations.* William Morrow. New York.

Hodder, I. 2006. *Çatalhöyük Research Project Volume 5.* McDonald Institute Monographs/ British Institute of Archaeology at Ankara.

Hölldobler, B. and Wilson, E. O. 2009. *The Superorganism.* W.W. Norton. New York.

Huntington, S. P. 1996. *The Clash of Civilizations and the Remaking of World Order.* Simon & Schuster. New York, NY.

Iberall, A., Wilkinson, D., and White, D. 1993. *Foundations for Social and Biological Evolution.* Cri-de-Coeur Press. Laguna Hills, CA.

Joos, G. 1950. *Theoretical Physics.* Hafner Publishing. New York.

Kroeber, A. L. 1944. *Configurations of Culture Growth.* University of California Press. Berkeley, CA.

Matthews, J. and Walker, R. L. 1964. *Mathematical Methods of Physics.* W. A. Benjamin. Reading, MA.

McGaughey, W. 2000. *Five Epochs of Civilization.* Thistlerose Publications. Milford, PA.

Mellaart, J. 1967. *Çatal Hüyük.* Thames and Hudson Ltd. London.

Melko, M. 1969. *The Nature of Civilizations.* Porter Sargent Publishers. Boston, MA.

Melko, M. and Scott, L. R. (eds). 1987. *The Boundaries of Civilizations in Space and Time.* University Press of America. Lantham, MD.

Moseley, M. E. 1992. *The Incas and their Ancestors.* Thames & Hudson. London.

Oppenheim, A. L. 1977. *Ancient Mesopotamia: Portrait of a Dead Civilization.* Univ. of Chicago Press. Chicago.
Pillsbury, J. 2006. *Moche Art and Archaeology in Ancient Peru.* National Gallery of Art – Studies in the History of Art. Washington DC.
Richardson, L. F. 1960. *Arms and Insecurity.* Quadrangle Books. Chicago, IL.
Roux, G. 1992. *Ancient Iraq.* Penguin Books. London.
Shklovskii, I. S., and Sagan, C. 1966. *Intelligent Life in the Universe.* Dell Publishing Co. New York, NY.
Simonton, D. K. 1984. *Genius, Creativity and Leadership.* Harvard University Press. Cambridge, MA.
Snyder, L. D. 1999. *Macro-History – A Theoretical Approach to Comparative World History.* The Edwin Mellin Press. Lewiston, NY.
Sorokin, Pitirim. 1941. *Social and Cultural Dynamics.* four volumes. Porter Sargent Publishers. Boston, MA.
_____. 1957. *Social and Cultural Dynamics.* Abridged. Porter Sargent Publishers. Boston.
Spengler, O. 1991. *The Decline of the West.* Oxford University Press. Oxford, UK.
Spiegel, M. R. 1964. *Theory and Problems of Complex Variables.* Schaum Publishing. New York.
Sperandeo, V. 1991. *Methods of a Wall Street Master.* John Wiley & Sons. New York.
Targowski, A. 2009. *Information Technology and Societal Development.* Information Science Reference. Hersey, PA.
Toynbee, A. J. 1961. *A Study of History.* Twelve volumes. Oxford University Press. Oxford, UK, 1934-61.
Toynbee, A. J. and Somervell, D. C. 1987a. *A Study of History Abridgement of Volumes I-VI.* Oxford University Press. Oxford, UK.
_____. 1987b. *A Study of History Abridgement of Volumes VII-X.* Oxford University Press. Oxford, UK.
Wheeler, William M. 1928. *The Social Insects: Their Origin and Evolution.* Harcourt Brace. New York.

INDEX

Abu Hureyra, 72, 73
Afghan, 19
Africa, 16
Aha, Pharaoh, 75
Akapana Pyramid, 63
al Qaeda, 19
Anatolia, 70, 71
Anatolian, 70, 73
Andean, 55, 56, 68
Anedjub, Pharaoh, 75
Aşikli Höyük, 70, 72, 73
tahuallpa, 65
Augustus Caesar, 38
bacteria, 4, 5
barbarians, 19
birth defects, 36
Bolivia, 62
border, effect of, 20
breakdown, 16, 17, 18, 20, 21
Breakdown, 65
Brown et al, 7
Cajamarca, 65
Calakmul, 48
Capacha Phase, 56
Caral, 60, 61, 62, 63, 65, 66, 67, 68, 70, 73
Casma, 61, 63, 65, 67
Çatalhöyük, 70, 72, 73, 84
Central America, 48, 53, 71
Chan Chan, 63
Chicama Valley, 65
Chile, 60, 62, 66

Chimú, 63, 67, 68
China, 17, 20, 21, 68, 71
Chincha, 62, 65, 67
Chinese, 17
Cival, 53, 55
civil wars, 6
Classical Mayan, 48, 49, 53, 54
Cold War, 16
Colima, 56
Communications, 3, 6
Creamer, W., 60, 61
culture, 16, 17, 18
Cuzco, 62, 65, 66
cyclic behavior, 2
decline, of West, 16
Den, Pharaoh, 75
Djer, Pharaoh, 75
Djet, Pharaoh, 75
drought, 53, 54, 63
Ebola, 24, 34, 44
Egypt, 68
El Mirador, 48, 55
El Niño, 63
El Salvador, 55
energetic principles, 2
energetics, 7, 10, 11
energetics/thermodynamics, 11
energy-based model, 7
Estrada-Belli, F., 50
Euphrates, 71, 72
Europe, 16, 20, 21, 71
free will, 12

Gazlake, P. S., 84
Giza, 60, 61
global warming, 14, 20, 21, 70, 71
Göbekli Tepe, 70, 72, 73
Great Zimbabwe, 84
Growth, 3, 6, 7, 10, 64, 78, 84
growth model, 7
growth phase, 16, 17, 18, 19, 20
Guatemala, 55, 56
Guatemalan Highlands, 55
Haas, J., 61
Hacilar, 72, 73
Hellenic civilization, 19, 65
Hesiod, 84
Hindu fundamentalist sub-society, 20
Hodder, 72, 84
Hodell, D., 48, 53
Hölldobler, 3, 4, 84
Horus cult, 77, 78
Huari, 62, 65, 67, 68
Huascar, 65
immigration, 16, 19, 20
imperfect superorganisms, 5, 6
Incas, 61, 62, 63, 65, 66, 67, 68, 84
India, 17, 18, 20, 21
Indonesia, 19
IndoTechnic civilization, 17, 20
Indus River Valley, 71
internal growth, 7, 8
interregnum, 18
Iraq, 19
ISIS, 23
Islam, 18, 19
Islamic civilization, 18, 19, 20
Islamic nation, 23
isolated, 61
Israel, 18, 19, 71
Japan, 16, 20
Japanese, 16, 20

Jerico, 70
Jordan, 71
Ka, King, 75
Konya Plain, 73
La Florida, 62, 65, 67, 68
Lambayeque River Valley, 63
Lebanon, 71
Lima, 60, 62, 63, 65
Lost World Pyramid, 55
Lotka, 11
Lower Egypt, 77
Machallilla, 56
Mayans, 53
Mayta Capac, 65
Mellaart, J., 84
Menes, Pharaoh, 75
Mersin, 73
Mesopotamia, 68, 85
Mexico, 55, 71
Middle East, 18
military, 16, 18, 19
Minchan Çaman, 63
Moche, 63, 64, 67, 68, 85
Moche Valley, 63
Mochica, 63
Muslim, 19
Musular, 72
Ñançen Pinco, 63
Napoleon, 14
Narmer Palette, 77
Narmer, Pharaoh, 75, 77
Neolithic, 70, 71, 72, 73
Nepeña River Valley, 63
Nile River civilization, 78, 79
Norte Chico, 60, 61
nuclear destruction, 16
nuclear proliferation, 16
Ocoña Valley, 65
Ocós, 56, 57, 58

oil, 18, 19
Olmecs, 58
Pachakuti 'Inka, 65
Pan Islamic Movement, 18
Panama, 55
pandemic, 24, 25, 44
Parita Bay, Panama, 55
Patavilca River Valley, 61
perfect superorganisms, 5
period, 16, 21
Peru, 60, 61, 62, 63, 65, 68, 70, 73, 84, 85
Petén, 55
PetroIslamic civilization, 18
Philippines, 19
Piramide Mayor, 61
Piura, 63
pollution, 36
ponerine ants, 5
population limitation, 37
Preclassical Mayan Civilization, 53, 54, 55
predecessor civilization, 75
progress, 16, 18
Qa'a, Pharaoh, 75, 77, 78
Qa'a Upheaval, 78
rally, 16, 20, 53
recycling, 37
Red Crown of Lower Egypt, 77
religion, 56, 61
reproductive power, 7
reproductive power model, 7
reproductive work, 7
resource acquisition, 7, 8
revolution, 18
Roman Empire, 19, 65
Rome, 19
rout, 16, 64
Ruiz, A., 61
Russia, 16, 18, 20, 21
Russian Revolution, 18
Russo-Japanese War, 16
RussoTechnic civilization, 18
San Bartolo, 55
Saña River, 63
Santa River, 63
Saturno, W., 55
science, 18, 20
Semerkhet Calamity, 78
Semerkhet, Pharaoh, 75, 77, 78
sequences of civilizations, 66, 70
Set, 77, 78
Shady, R., 60
Siberia, 20
Sinic, 75, 77
Sinic civilization, 77
SinoTechnic civilization, 17, 20
social insects, 2, 5, 47
Societal Level, 49, 50, 54, 61, 64, 65, 68, 76
South American, 55
species, human, 3, 4, 5, 10, 11
Staff god, 61
standard of living, vii, 17, 33, 35, 36, 38, 44
Startup, 48, 50, 53, 61, 63, 64, 65
Startup phase, 16, 17, 18
Suberde, 72
successor, 63, 65, 68
Sudan, 19
Supe River Valley, 60
SuperCivilizations, 6
superorganisms, 2, 3, 4, 5, 6, 7, 10, 11, 47, 68, 92

Syria, 71, 72
Taliban, 19
Tall As-Sultãn, 70
Technic civilization, 16, 20
technology, societal benefits, 16, 17, 18, 20
Teotihuacan, 48
terrorism, 19
thermodynamics, 7, 10
Third World, 16, 19, 20
Thupa 'Inka, 65
Tigris, 71
Tikal, 48, 55
time of troubles, 16, 17, 18, 20, 21
Tiwanaku, 62
Toynbee, Arnold, 85
Turkey, 70
United States, 16, 18, 19, 21
Universal State, 53, 61, 63, 65
Upper Egypt, 77
war, 16, 19, 21, 65
Western civilization, 18, 19, 20
White Crown of Upper Egypt, 77
World War I, 16, 21
World War II, 16
Yellow River Valley, 71
zero sum economy, 37
Zimbabwe, 84

About the Author

Stephen Blaha is an internationally known physicist with interests in Science, the Arts, and Technology. He had an Alfred P. Sloan Foundation scholarship in college. He received his Ph.D. in Physics from The Rockefeller University and has served on the faculties of several major universities. He was also a Member of the Technical Staff at Bell Laboratories, a manager at the Boston Globe Newspaper, a Director at Wang Laboratories, and President of Blaha Software Inc. and of Janus Associates Inc. (NH).

Among other achievements he was a co-discoverer of the "r potential" for heavy quark binding developing the first (and still the only demonstrable) non-abelian gauge theory with an "r" potential; first suggested the existence of topological structures in superfluid He-3; first proposed Yang-Mills theories would appear in condensed matter phenomena with non-scalar order parameters; first developed a grammar-based formalism for quantum computers and applied it to elementary particle theories; first developed a new form of quantum field theory without divergences (thus solving a major 60 year old problem that enabled a unified theory of the Standard Model and Quantum Gravity without divergences to be developed); first developed a formulation of complex Special and General Relativity based on analytic continuation from real space-time coordinates to complex coordinates; first developed a generalized non-homogeneous Robertson-Walker metric that enabled a quantum theory of the Big Bang to be developed without singularities at t = 0; first generalized Cauchy's theorem and Gauss' theorem to complex, curved multi-dimensional spaces; received Honorable Mention in the Gravity Research Foundation Essay Competition in 1978; first developed a physically acceptable theory of faster-than-light particles; first showed a universe with three complex spatial dimensions may be icosahedral; first derived a composition of extrema method in the Calculus of Variations; first quantitatively suggested that inflationary periods in the history of the universe were not needed; first proved Gödel's Theorem implies Nature must be quantum; first provided a new alternative to the Higgs Mechanism, and Higgs particles, to generate masses; first showed how to resolve logical paradoxes including Gödel's Undecidability Theorem by developing Operator Logic and Quantum Operator Logic; first developed a quantitative harmonic oscillator-like model of the life cycle, and interactions, of civilizations that is based on energetics (thermodynamics) with equations of the same form as those that describe superorganisms; and first developed an axiomatic derivation of the form of The Standard Model plus a Dark Particles sector from complex space-time coordinates and Asynchronous Logic. Faster than light particles are naturally a result of the Complex Lorentz group embodied in his extended Standard Model.

He has had a major impact on a succession of elementary particle theories: his Ph.D. thesis (1970), and papers, showed that quantum field theory calculations to all orders in ladder approximations could not give scaling deep inelastic electron-nucleon scattering. He later showed the eigenvalue equation for the fine structure constant α in Johnson-Baker-Willey QED had a zero at α = 1 not 1/137 by solving the Schwinger-Dyson equations to all orders in an approximation that agreed with exact results to 8th order in α thus ending interest in this theory. In 1979 at Prof. Ken Johnson's (MIT) suggestion he calculated the proton-neutron mass difference in the MIT bag model and found the result had the wrong sign reducing interest in the bag model. These results all appear in Physical Review papers. In the 2000's he repeatedly pointed out the shortcomings of SuperString theory and showed that The Standard Model's form could be derived from space-time geometry by an extension of space-time to complex-valued coordinates, and of the Lorentz group to the complex Lorentz group (which supports faster than light transformations and particles. This deeper space-time basis shows that the Extended Standard Model developed by Blaha has an origin in geometry and is the true theory of elementary particles.

More recently Blaha has developed a theory of the Multiverse based on a complex Euclidian 16-dimensional space that explains (using the Wheeler-DeWitt equation for quantum gravity generalized to complex-valued space-times) the origin of the Cosmological Constant, the origin for the spatial asymmetry of the Universe, and an understanding of the origin of the newly found Web of Galaxies (that links all the groups of galaxies) in our universe.

He also developed proposals for faster than light starships using quark-gluon ion drives and drives based on particle-antiparticle annihilation. He designed new types of starships, uniships, that could breach the fabric of our universe and enter the multiverse with a view towards travel to other universes. As part of this development of the Multiverse he showed that a 16-dimensional baryonic field could account for the major discrepancies in experimental measurements of G, the gravitational constant. This field enables uniships to escape from our universe. In addition to uniship engine designs he described a coherent baryonic field generator that is analogous to electromagnetic lasers.

In the early 1980's Blaha was also a pioneer in the development of UNIX for financial, scientific and Internet applications: benchmarked UNIX versions showing that block size was critical for UNIX performance, developed financial modeling software, started comparative database benchmarking studies, developed Internet-like UNIX networking (1982) and developed a hybrid shell programming technique (1982) that was a precursor to the PERL programming language. He was also the database manager of the AT&T ten-year future products development database. His work helped lead to commercial UNIX on computers such as Sun Micros, IBM AIX minis, and Apple computers.

In the 1980's he pioneered the development of PC Desktop Publishing on laser printers. and was nominated for three "Awards for Technical Excellence" in 1987 by PC Magazine for PC software products that he designed and developed.

In the past twelve years Dr. Blaha has written over 40 books on a wide range of topics. Some recent major works are: *From Asynchronous Logic to The Standard Model to Superflight to the Stars, All the Universe!,* All the Multiverse!, and *SuperCivilizations: Civilizations as Superorganisms.*

© S. Blaha 2014 All Rights Reserved.

© S. Blaha 2014 All Rights Reserved.

www.ingramcontent.com/pod-product-compliance
Ingram Content Group UK Ltd.
Pitfield, Milton Keynes, MK11 3LW, UK
UKHW050411240426
12048UKWH00020B/1465